Monetizing
Data

Monetizing Data

A Practical Roadmap for Framing, Pricing & Selling Your B2B Digital Offers

Stephan M. Liozu
Wolfgang Ulaga

Value Innoruption Advisors Publishing • Anthem AZ • 2018

Monetizing Data
A Practical Roadmap for Framing, Pricing & Selling Your B2B Digital Offers
By Stephan M. Liozu and Wolfgang Ulaga

Published by Value Innoruption Advisors Publishing
1946 W Eastman Court
Anthem, Arizona 85086
USA
www.valueinnoruption.com

ISBN: 978-1-945815-04-1 trade paperback
       978-1-945815-05-8 electronic book

First printing

Design and composition: www.dmargulis.com

MANUFACTURED IN THE UNITED STATES OF AMERICA

We dedicate this book to the digital B2B heroes who are changing the world and leading transformations courageously and pragmatically. We hope that this book guides them in their quest for success.

Contents

Preface

THE WORLD IS GOING digital, and there's no stopping the digital tsunami. Much has been written about digital transformation and about how this vast movement affects industries and firms. While most of the interest has been geared toward how companies can benefit from digitization for internal efficiency improvements, executives increasingly want to understand how business-to-business (B2B) companies can "turn data into revenue and profits."

With this book, we fill the gap of urgently needed practical guidelines for "monetizing data"—that is, for developing and commercializing new data-driven offers in B2B markets. Knowledge on selling data and analytics in the form of new digital market offerings is still in its infancy. Many firms are interested but want to know where and how to begin. Others have begun to experiment with digital pilots but are unsure how to grow and scale up their digital portfolio. Finally, a small number of firms can already look back on their own learning curve.

To achieve profitable growth and stand out among rapidly growing competition, it's no longer enough to simply test the waters.

Companies must begin to think more strategically about monetizing data, determine how to compete through innovative digital services that are unique, and different from next-best alternatives, and truly create *more* value for (and with!) business customers.

We wrote this book for the senior executives and experienced managers who want to design and implement a data monetization strategy that will deliver results. Whether you're in a general management position; in charge of business development, innovation, marketing, or pricing; or selling digital offers in B2B—this book is for you!

This book focuses on data monetization and on the value-based pricing of data-driven offers. In it we introduce a newly developed, practical roadmap for data monetization that can be used by digital project teams, incubators, and digital factories to better frame their offers and to apply the principles of value-based pricing. We present options in digital pricing models and practical guidelines for deploying them.

Our book takes you on a hands-on journey toward turning data into revenue and profits. Our roadmap will help you explore what customers really need and how you can create true customer value through data and analytics, and do so better than the competition. We discuss how you can generate unique insights through experimentation and pilot projects in close cooperation with customer pilots. Our book explains how fast commercial prototyping will allow you to identify and select the right pricing and sales approaches for your new digital offers.

In sum, we hope that our book proves helpful and thought-provoking. At the same time, we're aware that in this fast-moving domain, new insights and new knowledge are created every day. Thus, please consider this book as an intermediary milestone on your own journey to mastering data monetization. In the true spirit of knowledge co-creation, we do not have the ambition to provide a "final" answer to all challenges on your journey to profiting from data-driven revenue and profit growth. We're sincerely interested in your comments and reactions, and we hope that our book will initiate a fruitful dialogue among our community on this exciting topic. Please share your ideas with us. May we *co-create* the journey of monetizing data together!

Stephan M. Liozu
Thales
Stephan.LIOZU@us.thalesgroup.com
Sliozu@gmail.com

Wolfgang Ulaga
INSEAD, Europe Campus (France)
Wolfgang.Ulaga@insead.edu

Acknowledgments

THIS BOOK IS THE result of the many interviews, projects, and workshops we've conducted with companies around the globe. We've researched all the published reports on the topic from dozens of experts, consulting companies, and scholars. Yet, this exciting project would not have been possible without the help of the many executives and managers who've shared with us their experiences and insights along the way. Among many others, we thank in particular Avnet, Boeing, Caterpillar, Dell, Intel, Keysight Technologies, Pioneer, Signify, Siemens, Thales, Vallourec, Vixxo, and VWR.

We would like to thank our many contributors and the people who've inspired us to create this roadmap and the data monetization framework:

- Marie-France Crevecoeur, Signify
- Juliette Ulaga, Signify
- Joanna Gonos, Vixxo
- Warren Weller, Vixxo
- Richard Perrot, Thales InFlyt Experience

- Katie Richardson
- Peyton Marshall, LeveragePoint
- Marc Diouane, Zuora
- Halim Belkhatir, Zuora
- Dr. Titus Kehrmann, ConnectedValue
- Boris Galonske, ConnectedValue
- Todd Snelgrove, Experts in Value
- Emilie Saule

Monetizing
Data

Introduction

Digital is the main reason just over half of the companies on the Fortune 500 have disappeared since the year 2000.
—Pierre Nanterme, Accenture CEO

THE MARKET FOR DIGITAL business is worth trillions. If that strikes you as an exaggeration, read the mind-boggling estimates from some of the world's top consulting firms. KPMG forecasts an overall market value of $3.7 trillion for the Internet of Things (IoT) by 2020. The value created by the Industrial Internet of Things (IIoT) alone should reach $15 trillion by 2030, according to Accenture, which already sees annual spending on the IIoT hitting $500 billion in 2020 alone. To put those numbers in perspective: the gross domestic product of the United States is just under $20 trillion.

Massive growth and massive disruption are inevitable.

Like the gold rushes and oil rushes of centuries past, the promise of these numbers has mobilized a forceful response. We witness companies starting incubators, opening digital factories, and creating new divisions. The number and extent of digital transformations are accelerating. A digital tsunami is engulfing every industry. Realizing they need to take this development seriously, companies have three options: hide, immerse, or drown.

But the most fascinating aspect for us—as economies around the world prepare to be awash in trillions of dollars of digital value—is that many companies have yet to turn digital opportunities into solid revenues and profits. Many firms still struggle with quantifying, documenting, and communicating the value of digital offers. Very few companies excel in extracting the value of their digital through pricing. Only a few truly profit from digital, data-driven businesses, especially in manufacturing.

But it will happen for companies that take the right steps with the right level of digital maturity. The whole premise of this book is to help companies reach the next critical milestone on their digital transformation journey: how to monetize data. The 12 chapters in this book will help you understand, (co-)create, communicate, deliver, and capture more value from digital offers than your competition.

Let's be clear. Digital is so big and so different that it requires a new set of business practices. Twists on and tweaks to old models are doomed to fail. This book lays out the breadth and depth of this new form of business—data monetization—in detail. What you'll read here doesn't come out of thin air or theory. Instead, this book reflects the results of our work with dozens of firms and hundreds of executives and managers on how to derive *more* value from selling data-driven offers in business-to-business (B2B) markets. In addition, we've complemented our experience with thorough research on the latest reports from leading experts as well as our own interviews with industry leaders and analyses of best practices. You could say that we've done all the reading and interpretation for you—so that you don't have to—and then summarized it in a straightforward, accessible, hands-on road-map with visuals and step-by-step instructions.

In detail, we led well over 50 workshops with companies and reviewed over 250 reports published between 2012 and 2018 by consultants, governments, institutions, companies, and individual experts. We conducted qualitative interviews with 31 digital and pricing experts in 2016 and 2017 and surveyed decision makers as part of Arizona State University's annual Compete through Service symposium in 2016. Valuable insights also came from the executive roundtable on data-driven disruption in organizational frontlines during the Fourth Annual Organizational Frontlines Research Symposium (2018) and from ASU's Center for Services Leadership (CSL) Community of Practice on Monetizing Data and Analytics, reflecting cooperation between eight CSL member firms to share best practices in data monetization.

From working with firms, we've learned that a growing number of senior executives now ask more aggressively for a return on analytics, not only by using data to achieve internal efficiency gains but also by commercializing new data-enabled offers vis-à-vis customers. As one of the senior executives we worked with stated: "That's the […] credibility test. You really have to have a clear value proposition for the C-suite." Another manager added: "It's the Wild West right now. But how do you monetize that? How do you move that to a service model? It's a perfect storm; it's a new frontier." A third executive added: "Many people try and come out with this [new digital offers]. But there is more bullshit than reality. We see manufacturers fail. We see software companies make investments and leave the market because they had no clue of what they were doing."

Against this backdrop, we believe this book will raise digital awareness and maturity, and will become an essential tool and hands-on guidebook for practitioners, and for people working in digital incubators, digital businesses, and even core businesses.

Before we get to the individual chapters, though, we need to establish some definitions, describe the necessary changes to corporate DNA, dispel some myths, and explain why so many companies struggle to come to grips with this burning platform.

Redefining what *digital* means

When we talk about a digital platform, we're not talking about websites and social media and e-commerce. Understanding and leveraging what *digital* means in today's rapidly changing world requires a holistic view. We capture this in figure 0.1.

Our view in figure 0.1 makes two key points. First, we include elements such as data analytics and IoT. Second, we show that all elements are interconnected and work in unison. We use the term *digital maturity* to measure how well a company has understood and implemented this thinking. If a company is just entering into data analytics, and has an e-commerce platform and a website that look as if they've just arrived in a time capsule from the 1970s or the 1990s, that company lacks digital maturity.

Data monetization is not a box-checking exercise. Companies can claim that they already have everything shown in figure 0.1 to some extent, but that isn't sufficient. Selling goods online and collecting data from a few sensors in a product won't cut it. One thing our research made evident is that digital transformation requires a *corporate culture shift,* not just something that demands a different corporate culture.

Companies that don't quickly achieve a much higher level of digital maturity or fundamentally alter their corporate DNA are in trouble. Companies don't need us to tell them that the future will be in service and data, not manufacturing. This requires new

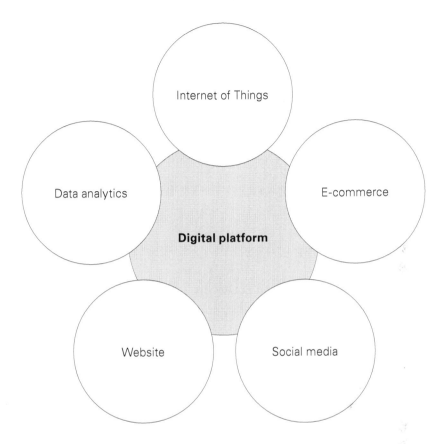

Figure 0.1. A holistic view of a digital platform.

business models and a dramatic shift in mindset. The speed is fast and driven by customers who are changing their behaviors. What we can help companies do is define and undertake the right steps to immerse in this tsunami—not hide or drown.

Change your corporate DNA—literally!

What does it mean to be a digital company? It was fascinating to hear the responses that came up a lot during our interviews. We can distill the sentiments of many respondents into a story like this:

> Most industries have a few big, traditional companies. Let's refer to them as dinosaurs. They have observed the situation, they have sensed the digital tsunami, and they think, "OK, how do I ride this wave?" They make a token attempt to acquire the trappings of digital. They launch an e-commerce website, they tell a new story to the marketplace, and maybe they introduce a new product with sensors that allow them to collect customer data. Then they make the claim that they're digital.

There are two problems digital immigrants face. First, as we said above, the trappings of digital are not sufficient. Second, no matter how they try to dress it up, the companies are still dinosaurs in their thinking, actions, resource allocations, and decision making.

What needs to change? Companies need to mutate themselves. They must inflict whatever it takes to re-engineer their corporate DNA. That is a prerequisite for what we're talking about in this book. We identify three specific mutations.

Mutation 1: Build for speed and agility

Are speed and agility part of your current corporate culture?

The combination of tremendous potential value, urgency, and speed to market means that companies face a catch-22 when they immerse themselves in digital: small bets won't make a big enough dent, but the necessary big bets can miss big. Imagine a company that's done nothing yet in terms of data monetization. Such a company faces the greatest risk that it will put its money into the wrong infrastructure and the wrong area of digital.

Speed and agility are essential, because digital value changes rapidly, both upward and downward. An example is Amazon in web services and cloud storage. The market is attractive, and the sense of urgency is growing. We see many companies jumping in, but the traditional, industrial companies aren't making the progress they expected because they lack the speed and agility to compete with Amazon. They compare themselves with other industrial companies and think they're doing well. But compared with digital natives, they're working at a snail's pace.

Mutation 2: Hone a "value survival instinct"

The challenges for companies in digital evolution are similar to those through billions of years of biological evolution. We can sum them up in one word: survival.

In digital business, that means answering the same fundamental questions that apply to any business:

- Where is the value in the data value chain?
- How much differentiation value do I have?
- How much do I want to capture through pricing?

What's changing is how a company answers those questions. Survival in the data monetization space requires a different instinct for customer value. Companies that have it and combine it with speed and agility will improve their chances of staying in the market or even reaching the top. This new instinct for value likewise requires a different perspective on how value is created and unlocked. Companies need to move away from the traditional marketing rules that may have served them well in the world of manufacturing and selling goods but that have no applicability to a data-driven service business. Companies have no choice but to move into the SAVE approach, away from the four keys of traditional product-oriented marketing strategies (product-price-promotion-placement). We show this approach in figure 0.2.

This is a solution-oriented model that includes software, data, content, media, and infrastructure. We refer to this model often in the book.

Mutation 3: Prepare for symbiosis

The days of arm's-length transactions with customers and suppliers and a "kill the competition" mentality are on the way out. They'll disappear with the dinosaur corporate DNA. Digital business takes place within value constellations, not along linear value chains. Successful companies will develop symbiotic relationships with suppliers and customers. In some cases, competitors will become future suppliers or customers, as the answers to the three "value survival instinct" questions shift.

The defining element in a value constellation is the customer. Companies will have to educate their customers about the switch from a transactional or even arm's-length relationship to one built on intense customer intimacy and interaction in a broader ecosystem. This is a transition through several stages and not

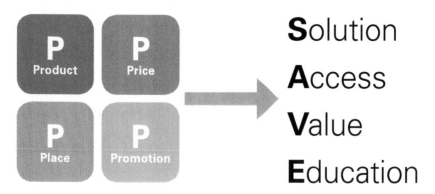

Figure 0.2. The SAVE model, which is replacing the traditional 4 P's approach to marketing.

something you simply switch *on*. Think of these steps as a series of modes through which customer relationships will evolve. The first is *partnership mode,* in which a company and its customers learn more about each other and redefine in more depth the customers' needs and how to meet them. Then the company and customers enter *co-creation mode,* in which the solution itself is developed together with the customer. Finally, they enter *experience mode,* when each customer realizes the true benefits of the solution designed exclusively for it and its needs. This results, of course, in a big shift in marketing, which the SAVE approach addresses.

One overlooked aspect of symbiosis is what takes place within the company itself! In a company that lacks digital maturity, the risk is high that the core business will reject integration of a new, data-driven model in the same way that a body rejects a transplanted organ. This rejection can deal a mortal blow to a company. Likewise, the company may have the surreal situation in which several digital platforms compete in isolation for similar parts of the value constellation. The core business and the ideas that emerge through incubators and co-creation with customers must have a symbiotic relationship, with the former leveraging its scale and infrastructure and the latter leveraging the new, deeper customer relationships. The various platforms in a company need to avoid redundancy and work together toward common goals.

Making these mutations will create a company prepared to win in digital monetization. But the effort to change old practices and discard misconceptions is not yet complete.

Seven "deadly" myths to overcome for data monetization

You cannot take a holistic approach to digital business, change your corporate culture, and undergo the mutations we just described if you buy in to the myths that surround and in some cases stifle attempts at launching a digital business. All these myths share the same undercurrent: that a company can become "digital" in the spirit of this book by bolting on individual digital aspects to their business, adding a sort of digital polish or sheen to the business, or sipping some digital Kool-Aid.

You can't.

Myth 1: Our current culture is "just fine"

Let's begin with culture. Many executives believe that "what brought us here will get us there." Many managers, especially in successful manufacturing-based firms, are proud of their company's history and achievements in a goods-centric environment. Yet, in light of the current massive transformations, it comes as a surprise that some companies still believe that a digital transformation, including data monetization, will occur without any accompanying cultural and/or people transformation. That isn't possible. What works in a traditional product-driven and transaction-driven company—from the boardroom to product development to sales to customer service—won't work for a digital business. Period.

In response, some companies feel that creating a digital factory or incubator means that they have made a digital transformation. That belief reveals an incomplete understanding of what *transformation* means. An incubator is, of course, an essential element in what we describe in this book, but it's a token gesture unless it's embedded in the right kind of organization. Similarly, adding sensors to a product does no more to qualify a company as a digital champion than owning a thermometer instantly makes someone a meteorologist. Anybody can invest $100 million in developers and start building apps.

We find it very telling that traditional goods-centric firms move quickly to creating "data factories." While such a choice of wording rightly reflects that, at some point, companies must industrialize digital offers to become profitable, the notion also signals a more problematic underlying worldview. Manufacturers are quick to move to the notion of "factory," a notion that is reassuring. A factory is a comfort zone for digital immigrants. Manufacturers know how to efficiently run a factory. But by quickly labeling their data-growth initiative a data factory, they also cement long-standing cultural beliefs.

But that will only bear a return if the company jumps into the most lucrative part of the value constellation, and at the right time. with the right business models.

Myth 2: Build it, and they will come

Executives in technology-driven firms often think that features will speak for themselves. "Having access to data and a really 'cool' algorithm will do the trick. Let's build a better data mousetrap, and customers will come." In this book we frequently return to an important theme: it isn't possible to have a successful business without customer intimacy. We devote an entire chapter to the topic early on, because it's the linchpin to the entire process. The concept of intimacy stretches far beyond ideas such as "knowing your customer" or being "customer-oriented." We could go so far as to say that the degree of customer intimacy is a source and measure of competitive advantage in the 21st century.

Myth 3: Digital business is a "product" business

Similar—and this relates to the first myth about cultural transformation—is the myth that a company can succeed in digital business without a service culture and service orientation. **Digital**

business is service—by definition. The two are insepara-
ble.[1] Often product managers are the organization agents driving
the digital opportunities in collaboration with the digital incubator. Product owners and traditional product managers may have
trouble focusing heavily on service-based business models.

Myth 4: We can reach digital maturity fast
The next three myths derive from the belief that the word *digital* is
either some form of magic, performance-enhancing pixie dust or
something easier to do than a traditional business. Neither could
be further from the truth. Some companies believe that they can
achieve a level of maturity quickly in their digital go-to-market
strategies, even though they lacked marketing and pricing maturity in the existing core go-to-market strategies. The mere shift
to digital won't make a company automatically better. Digital is
a fast-moving, high-stakes environment. But it's a journey, and
getting all the pieces right might require pivoting several times
along the way, as GE Digital is experiencing.

*Myth 5: Trust in our products can be easily transferred to
digital offers*
Similarly, some companies assume that the trust that customers
have developed in their product business is a transferable good; in
other words, those customers will by default trust the company
to deliver on service and data-driven opportunities. That's false.
Digital trust is earned and must be renewed constantly as companies engage with different stakeholders and players in the value
constellation.

(main text continues on page 17)

---

1   See Christian Kowalkowski and Wolfgang Ulaga's book *Service Strategy in
Action: A Practical Guide for Growing Your B2B Service and Solution Business*
(Columbia, SC: Service Strategy Press, 2017).

Value-Based Approach, *by GE Digital*

GE Digital (GED) is the leading software company for the Industrial Internet. By connecting machine data to software, apps, and analytics, GE Digital enables our industrial customers to operate faster, smarter, and more efficiently. At the center of GED's value proposition are the software blueprints that consume machine data and provide analytics to drive the desired outcomes for our customers. While cost-plus pricing has its limitations in most applications, in the data and software industry, where unit cost is often ambiguous, cost-plus pricing was clearly no option. That is why GED has been on a multiyear journey to become a value-based pricing and selling organization. Having a value-based pricing and selling strategy means that GED must price our solutions to deliver more value to our customers than our customers' alternatives and that our sales team can articulate and demonstrate the differentiated value that we deliver.

Enabling an organization to price and sell on value did not happen easily or quickly. The most critical aspects of the journey were the following:

1 *GED established a governance structure early, with senior leadership buy-in and participation.* The primary role of senior leadership is to do three things: set a winning strategy, hire and empower great teams to execute, and allocate capital to execute the strategy. Our Pricing and Value Steering Committee ensures that pricing policies, procedures, and roles of various stakeholders in the organization are aligned with business strategy.

2 *GED took as much time as necessary to ensure that a shared vision and a burning desire to transform to a value-based pricing and selling strategy existed among the teams.* For GED's value proposition to resonate with

customers and convince them that we offer the best value in the market, a cross-functional thread needed to exist, and that thread became customer value. Our product teams enhance and build the functionality that solves a customer problem and drives a differentiated offering. Marketing creates messaging, and sales plays around that differentiation specific to needs-based customer segments. Pricing takes stock of customer needs, cost to deliver, and the competition's offerings to establish the price that delivers the most value to customers at margins that reflect a differentiated offering. Sales delivers value-laden, articulate messaging to the customer.

3 Paramount to this last point, *GED established a value engineering team to support strategic transactions.* This team produces economic value estimates early in the sales cycle, which requires no data from the customer. By leveraging publicly available data, we demonstrate that we know the customer, the customer's business, and how we can deliver value for that customer. During the solutioning phase of the sales cycle, when required, this team leads a business case workshop where we perform a bottom-up validation of the economic value estimate (usually on site with the customer). Finally, during the negotiation phase, this team justifies the price vis-à-vis the business case that we co-create with the customer, our differentiated value, and the customer's next-best alternative. It is through this process that we ensure that GED will deliver the right solution for the right price that optimizes both the value and the time to value for the customer.

While we have much to celebrate, there is always more to accomplish, and GED continues to expand the deployment of value-based pricing and selling to more of the operations portfolio.

(continued from page 14)

Myth 6: Your salesforce will easily go digital

The sixth myth we often hear is the assertion that a company's current salesforce will automatically begin selling digital offers with new pricing models. The digital offers and the new pricing models are critical elements that require a significant reorientation and perhaps even an entirely new sales strategy, including an overhaul of sales goals, structures, processes, incentive systems, and people.

Myth 7: Every product will become a smart device

The final myth may seem counterintuitive at first. When business-people read that in a few years there will be many more things connected to the Internet than people (see data from Gartner, for example), it fosters a feeling that every product now needs to be "smart." We'd like to refute that myth as well. Not every product needs to be connected to the Internet. What matters, as we mentioned a moment ago, is customer intimacy and serving a customer's needs in the best and most sustainable way. A "smart" product is essential only if it helps complete that mission—in other words, if the "value survival instinct" calls for it.

Why data-driven business models are difficult ... and what you can do about it

No one said data monetization would be easy. What makes the job easier, though, is to understand and address or avoid the typical problems that crop up in data-driven models. Our expert interviews revealed much about where companies encounter difficulties. The most common difficulty is a misalignment between the core business strategy and the digital strategy. Whether the issue is a lack of integration or that the digital strategy is not fully embedded, a company cannot afford to have the digital strategy and the core business going in separate or even conflicting directions. Remember what we said above about symbiosis.

Then there are issues with organizational design. For example, should the incubator be outside the core as a separate company? Do you retrain salespeople or hire an entirely different salesforce for selling digital offers? When and how do you integrate digital opportunities into the core business? These questions trace their answers back to the understanding of value creation and customer relationships. Digital businesses exist within a value constellation, not along an old-fashioned value chain. It's really a total ecosystem. Success in any ecosystem depends on your choice of partners, your position within such a value constellation, and your willingness to accelerate your programs through open innovation. Get this wrong and the mistakes may be very hard to correct. Let's say you're a manufacturer of in-flight entertainment systems sold to commercial airlines. Your value constellation includes not only the hardware manufacturers, original content providers, and telecom and transportation service providers. You also need to learn to manage relationships with companies such as Netflix and Amazon, two entrants in this ecosystem that are moving very quickly and competently into content production to supplement their content distribution.

No company can afford to let someone else seize its partners and leave it out in the cold and out of its desired business. This is an extraordinary period in business evolution, as companies jockey for position and partners.

It comes as no surprise, then, that the phrase *business as usual* has no place in this new era. Your existing innovation, customer segmentation, and marketing processes will need to undergo considerable change, to the extent that they are applicable at all. The necessary approach is **customer "pull"** based on users' needs, not the traditional **technology-driven "push"** thinking that has predominated for decades. If you have a data-product-first approach to innovation (i.e., here are "cool" analyses and some algorithms—want to have some?), price them using a cost-plus approach, and do your segmentation after the fact, your company will be lost in the data-driven world of digital business. Relying on push versus pull is flawed even when you have the foresight to know the kinds of businesses that are emerging.

Many established companies are in a precarious position if they cling to a not-invented-here culture. The fact that they have large staffs of engineers and software developers lulls them into believing that they can "win" in digital on their own. They place less emphasis on partnerships and on the ability to scale rapidly. The time lost or wasted by relying solely on one's own strengths can be devastating. It can take two to three years to design, test, and scale a new software product, but in the meantime, competitors are forging partnerships in a different software ecosystem and embracing solutions based on accepted standards. Losing two or three years of digital time is huge.

An equally lethal killer is a lack of differentiation. When every company seems to be seeking its slice of the anticipated trillions from digital business, many are forgetting a question so fundamental that it inspired the title of one of Stephan's books: what makes you *different*? In the quest to tap into one's own strengths and meet the customer's urgent needs, a company can lapse into the dangerous combination of overconfidence and myopia. In other words, if you have too much faith in your own abilities and focus solely on customers without context, you risk losing sight of your numerous competitors who are pursuing similar goals. You lose sight of differentiation. The challenge is not to fulfill customer needs in absolute terms. The challenge is to fulfill customer needs sustainably better than anyone else, that is, in relative terms. Doing so is not possible without a tested, vetted superior value proposition.

When we encounter people working in incubators, the excitement is palpable. But the more we listen to companies talk about IoT, predictive maintenance, user needs, cloudification, and other trends in either general or absolute terms, the more we wonder about what those companies' competitors are up to and what conversations they're having with customers. If a company knew that five other companies were chasing after the same spot in the value constellation, and that differentiation would be minimal, would they still invest in that service? A digital market filled with multiple competitors with little differentiation will lead to the same outcomes as in the physical world: a "red ocean" with a commoditized race to the bottom and price as the main differentiation factor.[2]

This is what happens when you work in a vacuum. We summarize the facts behind this burning platform in figure 0.3.

Summary

The estimated value of digital markets is so vast that everyone is legitimately wondering how to enter. We're witnessing a tsunami of investment and a tsunami of activity. But the intriguing result is that very few companies have found a sweet spot yet. Across many industries we still have to set a new standard for sustainable profitability through data monetization.

Digital transformation affects the entire organization and many business processes. Many firms must learn how to create and

---

2   See also W. Chan Kim and Renee Mauborgne's book *Blue Ocean Shift: Beyond Competing: Proven Steps to Inspire Confidence and Seize New Growth* (New York: Hachette, 2017).

Burning value platform for digital programs

- The speed of hardware **obsolescence** is accelerating.
- Cost decreases in technology are **transparent**.
- Buyers are better trained and more **professional**.
- Buyers are **de-bundling** digital offers (hardware/software/data) to drive costs down.
- Your **competitors** are also investing in digital platforms.
- Part of the data value chain has been **commoditized**.

Digital offers cannot be designed and launched with a cost-plus approach!

Figure 0.3. The causes behind the burning value platform.

implement entirely new business models that often are incompatible with well-established business practices and traditional organizational models. Even though many companies have made significant inroads into the digital space, many still ask how to correctly "package" commercial offers around data and analytics so that they derive revenues and profitability from these offers. This book provides a roadmap and individual steps for mastering the journey toward data monetization.

Roadmap to Data Monetization

The prospects for pure hardware suppliers are not good in Competition 4.0. Fewer possibilities for differentiation will lead to declining margins and cutthroat competition. Unique selling points are really only possible with software or through innovation in the business model.

—Roland Berger's COO Insights *2016*

THIS ISN'T A BOOK on data, data transformation, or the technical side of the data business. It's also not a book on digital transformation; nor is it a pricing book. This is a book on data monetization. Everything that you'll read in this book is part of the data monetization process.

How to define data monetization? Monetizing data is related to—yet also slightly differs from—other key issues in B2B industries. For example, data monetization reaches beyond value-based marketing and sales, an area in which Wolfgang has published extensively. Likewise, monetization also differs from dollarization (see Stephan's book *Dollarizing Differentiation Value*). As we'll see, data monetization builds on value-based marketing and dollarization principles to add one further step.

To monetize data is to convert an asset into a revenue stream and profit by creating superior quantified financial value for customers, relative to competition. As figure 1.1 describes, you turn the data you collect into insights and actionable activities, then you create sources of revenue, and then you are paid by either a subscription, outcome, or pay-per-use model.

In many business markets, pricing of goods and services is 90 percent about understanding, documenting, and communicating value and only 10 percent about selecting the appropriate pricing model. That balance is more complicated with data, because

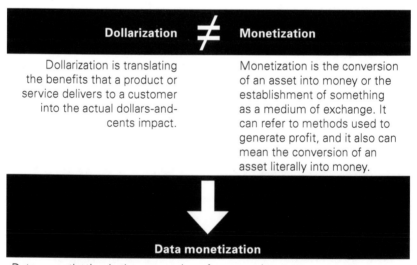

Dollarization ≠ **Monetization**

Dollarization is translating the benefits that a product or service delivers to a customer into the actual dollars-and-cents impact.

Monetization is the conversion of an asset into money or the establishment of something as a medium of exchange. It can refer to methods used to generate profit, and it also can mean the conversion of an asset literally into money.

Data monetization

Data monetization is the conversion of an asset into a revenue stream or into profit by creating greater quantified financial value for customers than your competition does.

Figure 1.1. Definitional clarity.

in digital B2B offerings, you have many more options for selecting a pricing model. For reference's sake, we would say that in the digital world, you still have to do 60 to 70 percent of the work on value, but you'll have to answer many more challenging questions around pricing. These include the testing and the risk management of pricing.

(*main text continues on page 28*)

Research Meets Practice: Key Insights

In February 2018 senior executives and scholars from around the globe came together in New Orleans, during the Fourth Annual Organizational Frontlines Research (OFR) Symposium, to discuss, among other topics, pressing managerial challenges and research priorities on how firms can best profit from monetizing data in business-to-business (B2B) markets. One of the four conference roundtables discussed findings of a five-month Delphi study conducted to gain insights from 11 experts in academia and management on how data-driven disruption will affect B2B companies and help them grow revenues and profits from data over the next years.[1]

Experts agreed that the growing use of data and analytics in B2B markets fundamentally affects existing ecosystems of customers, suppliers, channel intermediaries, and other stakeholders. In line with the Gartner Group's definition of digital disruption—"an effect that changes the fundamental expectations and behaviors in a culture, market, industry or

---

[1]   The study was coordinated by Wolfgang Ulaga (INSEAD) and Thomas Ritter (Copenhagen Business School) in cooperation with Sundar Bharadwaj (University of Georgia), Michael Brady (Florida State University), Gary Bridge (Snow Creek Advisors LLC), Douglas Herman (Ingram Micro), Ming-Hui Huang (National Taiwan University), Son Lam (University of Georgia), Rusty Martin (Porex, Filtration Group), Lisa Scheer (University of Missouri), and W. (Michel) van der Borgh (Copenhagen Business School).

process that is caused by, or expressed through, digital capabilities, channels or assets"[2]—experts discussed three major emerging topics related to data monetization: (1) the impact on existing relationships between firms and the creation of new interfirm ties, (2) the growing expectations among key decision makers for documenting return on investment (ROI) of data monetization initiatives, and (3) the emergence of new key factors of success for achieving revenue and profit growth through data monetization.

First, experts agreed that firms' growing emphasis on monetizing data in their respective markets will reshape business relationships among all actors involved in B2B ecosystems. The growing use of data triggers the emergence of entirely new relationships and threatens the existence of established ties between firms. Data further strengthens or weakens existing interactions. Decision makers must understand the forces that shape these business relationships and learn how to use enablers, such as commitment, power, and trust, to navigate within these changing value constellations, while taking into account new ethical and legal considerations emerging from a growing presence of data and analytics in business markets.

Second, practitioners and academics agreed that—after a first wave of excitement about data and digital transformation—decision makers now raise hard questions regarding financial returns derived from data monetization initiatives. Early on, executives often considered such initiatives as experiments, aimed at building a learning curve, or quickly declared them successful, without scrutinizing performance outcomes. Now executives increasingly ask for ROI.

Experts agreed that the growing use of data across industries bears a potential for unleashing new opportunities to

---

2   https://www.gartner.com/it-glossary/digital-disruption

generate revenues and profitability through data and analytics. Yet, efforts aimed at monetizing data also bear risks of value destruction. Roundtable experts explained that there are clearly "winners and losers" when it comes to profiting from data monetization. As the cards are redistributed through shifting power, some firms are definitely better placed than others for *both creating and capturing incremental value through data.* Participants discussed examples of data power shifts in industries where firms struggled to gain access to (and control of) data, thus building new sustainable competitive data advantages as a prerequisite to securing new revenues and profits. For example, by focusing on new offers built solely around data, new entrants tackled established positions held by incumbent manufacturers and threatened established customer relationships with entirely new value propositions. Clearly, competition between digital natives and digital immigrants in many markets not only triggers new opportunities for value creation; it also creates new risks of value destruction.

Third, to understand which firms are best positioned to profit from data monetization, experts pointed to the emergence of new success factors. While the sheer existence of data initially seemed to justify in itself the development of new offerings, there is growing evidence that innovative data-driven offers must increasingly rely on a diverse set of unique resources and distinctive capabilities to master data monetization. Examples are low-cost sensors, competitive costs of data transmissions, a steep decline in data storage costs, new (and often free) analytical tools, and advances in visualization techniques, to name just a few.

Collectively, the three themes described above set the stage for developing the roadmap to successful data monetization described in this book. The following chapters discuss the key milestones of this transformational journey.

(*continued from page 25*)

Data monetization begins
with a good business model

The first prerequisite for successful data monetization is the business model. Many companies encounter problems because they try to work the process in the wrong direction by beginning with the pricing model. Figure 1.2 shows the proper sequence.

Our experience working with numerous industrial companies and their digital teams reveals that teams have preconceived notions about pricing in the digital space. Because digital staff are buyers of digital services themselves, they quickly jump to what they know in the business-to-consumer (B2C) world as consumers. It's not unusual to hear teams select freemium pricing as a de facto model for their B2B pricing model. Freemium is known

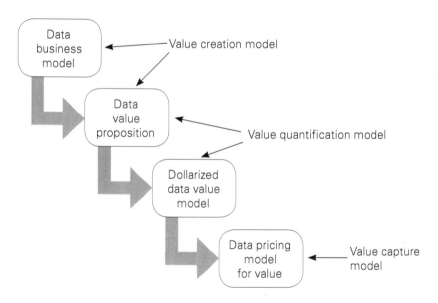

Figure 1.2. The first prerequisite for successful data monetization is the business model.

in digital B2C and is also easier to conceptualize. But freemium and other pricing models cannot be disconnected from the overall business model and the segmentation strategy. We talk more about this in the chapter on pricing models.

So it's important to guide the digital teams through the sequence of data monetization (shown in figure 1.3) and to reinforce that each step in the sequence is critical to selecting and designing the right pricing model(s).

When companies try to short-circuit this process, we ask them to show us their business model and their customer value proposition. You really need clarity around each of these buckets, in the right sequence. You can't skip steps, because there's a logic to this sequence. Only after you've begun with value creation, dollarized your value, and defined the value pool will you be able to understand how much potential value you create for customers and how much you could capture. Likewise, only then can you make

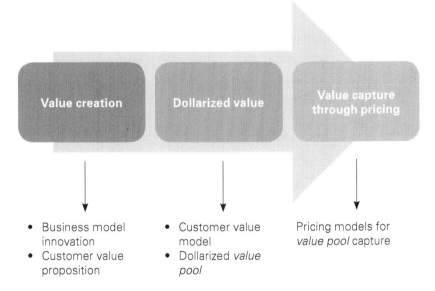

Figure 1.3. The sequence of data monetization.

a robust decision about whether to stay with a traditional pricing model or whether to innovate with a long-term, recurring revenue model (subscription), or pay-per-use, or performance sharing.

The importance of testing your value hypotheses ... internally!

A performance claim that you've validated internally is invaluable. We recommend that companies test everything internally when they begin the data monetization process. Imagine when you try to sell your service that you could tell your customers that you tested, vetted, and validated the concept in 20 of your own plants and saved 15 percent on maintenance costs. Then you give them the data and take them through the case study. This engenders a different level of trust than merely hypothesizing that you can save the customer 15 percent and trying to persuade them to test that together with you. Whenever possible, be your own guinea pig rather than putting the customer's business at risk as well. Services built around IoT or predictive maintenance lend themselves especially well to internal testing to demonstrate and document the value created. Far too few companies do this, though.

Once you know the real amount of value you can create, you can think about monetization models. A recent article in the *MIT Sloan Management Review* proposed three typical monetization models, as we show in figure 1.4. You can become a seller of data or a data broker, because you've seen the value of the data internally and you know that it brings value to someone in the data value chain. Most companies don't want to sell data or don't see a fit in becoming a data bank, but it's an option. The second option is to create totally new revenue streams through subscriptions or through a new business or service model. These kinds of incremental or additional models are often truly new in the

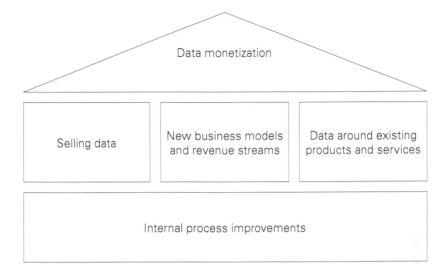

Figure 1.4. Models for data monetization. Based on Barbara H. Wixom and Jeanne W. Ross, "How to Monetize Your Data," *MIT Sloan Management Review,* January 9, 2017.

B2B industrial world, with no precedent within the company. The third option is to wrap data around your existing products and services and to offer optimization or services such as predictive maintenance. You are enriching your data and your products and services, and thus enriching the customer experience.

Regardless of which choice is best, before you go out and talk to anyone, you need to test the ideas internally. Take one of your plants or one of your assets, equip it, hypothesize about the savings, and then learn and document how it works. That's the foundation of the data monetization process. It might take a few months or a few years, but it's essential to be equipped with success stories in front of future pilot customers. When we talk about customer trust—we devote an entire chapter to it later—this kind of testing matters. If you don't do it, your customers might perceive as theoretical or hypothetical all the things you show them.

The seemingly endless options for monetization

Cars offer an excellent illustration of the many creative and potentially lucrative ways that a company can monetize data. Think of car-sharing business models, assisted driving features, the self-driving car, onboard entertainment, and so forth. All these applications have demonstrated value. McKinsey estimates the market for data-enabled services in automobiles to be between $450 billion and $750 billion by 2030.[3]

Now ... how do you price this? You could include data in the price of the equipment. You could charge a one-off payment, or you could charge a subscription for data for, say, entertainment in the car. You could monetize the content through advertising, or you could use a points or credit system. We summarize some of these possibilities in figure 1.5. These go a step beyond the options defined in figure 1.4.

The B2B digital world needs to learn rapidly from what's happening in the B2C world, where many of these innovative models are already familiar and desirable experiences. Who doesn't have a subscription to something? Consumers are also familiar with pay-per-use or payment based on performance. The Boston Consulting Group (BCG) echoed this in a report that lists seven points to keep in mind when trying to capture the value of digital services.[4] The process, of course, begins with customers and potential partners. A company needs to identify the stakeholders in its value constellation, understand how value is created, and listen to what customers expect from the service model. The BCG article also urges bolder pricing models, because traditional legacy models will probably provide insufficient protection or flexibility in the face of potential price erosion.

---

3   McKinsey & Company, *Monetizing Car Data*, September 2016.
4   Boston Consulting Group, "How the Internet of Things Will Change the Pricing of Things," December 7, 2017.

Data monetization options for connected cars	Pricing model options
Rolled into the price of the equipment	• Transactional product pricing • Premium-based product pricing
Charged as a one-off payment after the purchase or through aftermarket sales	• Transactional service pricing • Modular pricing (price menu)
Charged as subscription	• Subscription-based pricing
Covered by monetizing tailored advertising pushed to the end customers or elaborating, analyzing, and reselling data generated by these use cases	• Pay-per-use pricing • Outcome-based pricing
Deducted or debited from a rechargeable credit, as offered for selected content downloads	• Pay-per-use pricing

Figure 1.5. Examples of data monetization. Adapted from McKinsey & Company, "Monetizing Car Data," September 2016.

In a traditional go-to-market model, opportunities for capturing value may be two or three levels removed from an industrial manufacturer, who must understand where these pockets of value are and how to gain access to them. That is why direct access—rather than placement or distribution—is one of the marketing pillars in the SAVE model that we described in the introduction. In many business markets, manufacturers typically rely on indirect distribution channels: they reach business customers through distributors or other channel partners. While such go-to-market models benefit from obvious advantages in many ways (fast market coverage, asset-light expansion, etc.), they also represent a major obstacle to growing revenues and profits from digital offers. As we will see, in the digital space, B2B companies must secure direct access to both their direct and indirect customers.

Shifting from a cost focus to a benefit focus

Business customers source goods and services of other firms *for one reason only*: they need them in their own business processes. And there's only one rule for staying on top of the game among suppliers: our goods and services must provide better outcomes and enable customer processes more effectively and efficiently than the competition—as perceived by our customers.

Against this backdrop, providing better outcomes than a competitor for the same cost as or lower cost than the competition, while meeting quality expectations, resonates immediately with customers. Promising lower costs is often the easiest and most reliable way to get a foot in the door. Customers will listen when you claim that you can reduce spare-parts inventories, increase rotation, and so on. Beyond spot reductions, the theme of lower costs leads to the idea of total cost of ownership (TCO). But the next evolution of this idea is total benefits of ownership (TBO), which incorporates not only the benefits through cost savings over a product's lifetime but also the potential upside benefits to the customer through increased revenues.

Figure 1.6 shows some examples of the revenue upside from IoT and data-driven offers, depending on the source of value. Because it ties these benefits to innovative forms of value creation and shows sources of potential cost savings, TBO is superior for framing the value proposition of a solution and developing a pricing model than TCO alone.

Companies can generate more revenue through ensuring customer satisfaction, earning repeat business, offering service contracts, upselling customers by starting with a basic product or service and moving to a premium, and increasing market share. Granted, the long history of B2B industrial negotiation gives an advantage to monetizing the cost story. Most companies' skill sets

Create customer value	Lower costs	Increase revenues
Connect to smart machine to improve service and repair operations	• Decrease field visits • Reduce software update costs • Reduce time-to-fix and downtime • Reduce maintenance costs	• Improve customer satisfaction • Increase repeat business • Enable premium SLA service contracts • Improve upsell capabilities
Analyze IoT data to improve product design, reliability, and preventive actions	• Reduce warranty claims • Reduce number of service calls • Increase first-time fix rates • Reduce inventory costs • Improve quoting time and costs	• Increase market share • Increase quality and brand reputation • Reduce R&D delays and time to market • Improve forecasting ability and product availability
Transform your business with new innovative products and services	• Optimize R&D costs • Reduce number and time of support calls • Enable self-service support • Collaboration and information sharing	• Design premium and tailored offerings • New pay-per-use revenue models • New service/content subscriptions • Leasing/trade-in services

Figure 1.6. The sources of upside, which makes the difference between TBO and TCO. Adapted from IndustryWeek Webinar, "Autodesk IoT Survey," 2017.

and communication collateral emphasize that. It will take some adjustment and a special set of talents and skills to enable a company to understand and leverage TBO. It's a different negotiation when you can tell customers that you can support their efforts in marketing, customer satisfaction, and repeat business. It's also a more nuanced argument because the benefits, in contrast to cost reductions, aren't always easy to identify and translate into dollars and cents.

The overarching message here is that we've just scratched the surface on the vast opportunities for value creation. The more data that a company collects, and the better it gets at managing that data—that is, turning data into insight, and insights into action—the greater and more lucrative its opportunities should be. To unlock these opportunities, we recommend that managers follow the eight steps shown in figure 1.7, which form the core of this book. Some of these steps resemble those of value-based pricing processes. However, our roadmap for successfully mastering data monetization is not about pricing digital B2B offerings, even though several of our steps deeply relate to capturing value through pricing. This is your Data Monetization Roadmap. By tackling the key issues in each of our eight stages, you'll be able to define and implement your company's path to profiting from data monetization.

Data Monetization Roadmap

Step 1 Map your value constellation
Step 2 Revisit your customer segmentation
Step 3 Select the right pilot customers
Step 4 Put your offer in co-incubation with customers
Step 5 Measure and quantify the value of your solution
Step 6 Select and execute the right pricing model(s)
Step 7 Execute your pricing strategy through contracts and SLAs
Step 8 Transfer and scale the opportunity into the core business

Figure 1.7. The eight steps in the Data Monetization Roadmap.

Step 1: Map your value constellation. It's impossible to get deep into data monetization, the way we've designed it, without first paying considerable attention to your value constellation. You need a thorough understanding of what happens in the entire value constellation, which could even mean studying your customers' customers—and even customers further downstream. For example, when Intel began to investigate opportunities for offering IoT services in one particularly attractive industry vertical, fashion retailing, the semiconductor manufacturer quickly realized it had to gain deeper insights into the needs of textile manufacturers, fashion retailers, and even consumers (see our discussion in chapter 2). This task is particularly challenging in markets where your core (physical) business relies on distribution, which means you lack direct access to customers and their value chains. The detailed analysis of your value constellation helps you identify key *value enablers* and *value bottlenecks* that might be relevant to your digital success. They might also be critical to your business model design.

Step 2: Revisit your customer segmentation. In the digital world, your existing customer segmentation (assuming you have one in place and operationalized) will change. If you're planning to serve your traditional customers with your data-based digital services, you'll have to review and potentially adjust that existing segmentation because needs, costs, benefits, and willingness to pay will certainly shift. If you plan to enter a new market with a new digital opportunity, you're starting from scratch and will need a robust segmentation defined around an established and limited set of selection criteria. In that case it's even more essential to select the right end-use applications and the right customers and to focus on the primary differentiators. Focus is indispensable. You can't be scattered and look at hundreds of buyers for hundreds of potential end uses.

Step 3: Select the right pilot customers. Steps 1 and 2 are foundational in this new data-driven world to focusing on the right partnerships, the right customer segments, and the right end-use applications. In the end, these steps are done to be able to hand-pick the right customers to run deep pilots with. You need a structured and balanced process for selecting a portfolio of pilot customers based on the right criteria and not on close relationships or past business relationships. In digital and data, the first pilots need to demonstrate the feasibility, desirability, and viability of your minimum viable product (MVP) or digital offer.

Step 4: Co-incubation. In incubation with customers, you jointly develop a concept of your digital offer using techniques such as fast prototyping and developing MVPs. Each customer is different, different assets with different life cycles are involved, manufacturing processes vary, and different types of data are required. We cannot underline enough the importance of Step 4, because many great ideas are put to the test at this critical stage. Cisco claimed in 2017 that 60 percent of IoT initiatives stall in the proof-of-concept stage, and that only 26 percent of companies have had an IoT initiative they consider a success.[5]

Step 5: Measure and quantify value. The next step on our roadmap gets to the heart of value-based pricing: identifying value drivers, quantifying value opportunities, and documenting value created. In this book, we dedicate a chapter to pricing of data-driven offers, in which we describe our own approach to dollarizing value and setting prices for such offers. Step 5 is so crucial, and yet so shockingly neglected in many instances, that we feel we must emphasize one of the most important points of data monetization. This may be one of the most important points in the entire book:

---

5   "Nearly 3/4th of Internet of Things Projects Are Failing: Cisco," *Economic Times,* May 27, 2017.

Your customers aren't static. They're not in some happy state of suspended animation, waiting for you to bring your brilliant innovative solution to their doorstep. Business customers are permanently screening the market for alternative suppliers, talking with your active and agile competitors, and making constant comparisons.

If you're not aware of what your customers and your competitors are doing, you're in trouble!

Step 6: Select and execute your pricing model. To facilitate your way through Step 6 of the roadmap, we reviewed extant pricing literature, discussed pricing choices with multiple managers, and developed four options for you to choose from. This means we've cut through the potentially confusing and seemingly endless array of pricing models that (legitimately) exist in the digital world. These options, which everyone is focused on, are as follows:

- traditional product pricing
- subscription-based pricing
- outcome-based pricing
- pay-per-use pricing models

Each of the four options we discuss comes with its own barriers, pros and cons, best practices, success stories, and cautionary tales, which we explore in detail in chapter 9.

Step 7: Execute your pricing strategy. This step is a reminder that the work is by no means finished when you've selected a pricing model. How do you turn that pricing approach into a contract? Price negotiations are much different now. Like the pricing challenges emerging from manufacturers' move from a goods-centric to a service-centric pricing and sales model, companies must learn how to execute pricing decisions when moving from services deeper into digitally driven combinations of goods and services. Remember what we said in the introduction. With the growing role of "data as a service" (data *is* service), you need to approach customers differently when it comes to pricing. You don't engage customers with a pay-per-use or outcome-based pricing model or business model the same way that you engage them under a transactional model. What matters now are service, monitoring, reporting, and engaging your customers. You need the right organization, the right contracts in place, and the right service mindset.

Step 8: Transfer your digital business back to the core. The final step is to transfer the business from the incubator back to the core business, with all the cultural and commercial implications that brings. What are the right roles and responsibilities? What are the pricing guidelines? Who will make sure the business plan is implemented? Who is responsible for scaling the new business, and how will they accomplish that?

Two things make this digital world especially fascinating for us. First, no one has found a sweet spot in terms of monetizing data in the best possible way, even though some have been searching for almost two decades. In this book we claim that there can and should be a better financial outcome of your digital offers. In the end, the simplest questions are often the most challenging and therefore go unanswered. In this digital world, which revolves around customer intimacy, what makes you unique? Why should a customer pick you? You have 20 competitors asking the same questions, so how will you come out ahead?

When we ask these simple questions, we're often greeted with silence. Then we name a competitor who we know is talking to their customers, and we ask why would a customer pick *them*? Again, silence.

Companies need to find bold answers to these questions. And that leads to the second fascinating aspect for us. Digital is really the meteor hitting the B2B industrial world. Size and experience and a long history as a traditional business do not translate into automatic success in the digital world. As a GE executive told *MIT Sloan Management Review* in 2016, "The work of connecting and monitoring large volumes of real-time data is not our core strength."[6]

Analogous to the dinosaurs 65 million years ago, we see both sides of this event. Yes, we could focus on the mass extinction of incumbents. But mass extinction creates mass opportunity! Much more important and compelling are the stories the survivors will tell. Who will evolve and emerge as the new dominant players? What opportunities do they have for rapid proliferation?

Think of this book as your own radiation lamp to mutate your corporate DNA so that you can survive this meteor strike and capitalize on the trillions of dollars of opportunities it leaves behind. You now have a roadmap to help. In the next chapter, we explore in greater detail what customer intimacy means in the context of monetizing innovative offers in B2B markets as we let the roadmap guide us on this journey together.

---

6   Laura Winig, "GE's Big Bet on Data and Analytics," *MIT Sloan Management Review*, February 18, 2016.

2

The Heart of the Matter Is Customer Intimacy

*Your **customers** are the judge, jury, and executioner of your value proposition. They will be merciless if you don't find fit! Companies should focus on one of three value disciplines: operational excellence, product leadership, or **customer intimacy**.*

—Alex Osterwalder

CUSTOMER INTIMACY IS THE most important prerequisite for successfully monetizing data. We've said already that customer intimacy reaches far beyond the usual knowledge of customers, their business operations, and their key contacts. *Customer intimacy* refers to a deep understanding of customers' business model, insights into how customers "make money," and the ability to translate those insights into helping customers run their own business more effectively and efficiently. Customer intimacy allows suppliers to help customers eliminate unnecessary costs, achieve better results, and serve their own customers in better, smarter ways. In short, customer intimacy is a key lever for making a lasting impact on customers' top- and bottom-line results.

Customer intimacy means unifying *push* and *pull*

As in many other instances, we've seen B2B companies fall into the classic trap of concentrating all efforts on "selling features" rather than building digital offers from the ground up—that is, beginning with a simple question: Where's the value for customers? What do they want to achieve? When companies begin the journey of commercializing new data-enabled offers, they risk falling in the traditional "techno push" versus "market pull" trap. Too many firms try to push data-enabled services or sensor-ready products onto their customers, simply because it's technically possible to offer such products and services. These firms don't distinguish between what's technologically *possible* and what's actually *valuable*—from a customer perspective.

The temptation to rely on techno push in the data space is omnipresent because it's easier and faster. When a company owns data or has direct access to it, develops proprietary algorithms to analyze and interpret it, and then packages an offer around it, it's tempting to believe that data plus a number of "cool" analyses will fly off the shelves, no questions asked. In working with companies on commercializing data, we've seen, more than once, that executives believe that such offers sell themselves: build it, and they will come. Customers will automatically see the value.

In data monetization in particular, companies must understand that having unique resources (data) and distinctive competencies (analytics) is only half the equation. To succeed, firms must embrace data-as-a-service and focus on the true north: to develop a value proposition that truly resonates with customers, firms must understand why and how data creates value for customers. And eventually they have to understand how they can monetize better than their competition!

Yet there also is a need to strike the right balance. The classic dichotomy between techno push and market pull might sound like an either-or choice, with market pull preferable because it means customers desire and seek out something that will help them solve their problems. Data monetization often changes that dynamic. We've seen multiple situations where suppliers ultimately knew more about customers and their operations themselves. They didn't have to ask, interview, or observe customers. With customer data in hand, suppliers could start a dialogue they hadn't had with customers before. We therefore argue that a company needs an assertive approach that depends on *both* techno push and market pull. Like what happens when two powerful magnets meet, you need to make sure that an unbreakable bond forms between you and your customer where pull meets push.

Data-driven B2B offers begin with defining your customer's *job to be done*

What are the fundamental problems that a customer wants to solve? What are the ultimate performance metrics that "rock the boat" with a business customer? To understand what really matters to our customers, we refer to a notion coined by Clayton Christensen: the *job to be done.* In a 2007 article he coauthored in *MIT Sloan Management Review,* he defined a job to be done as "the fundamental problem a customer needs to resolve in a given situation."[7] But when we talk about data, there are multitudes of ways to understand and resolve the job to be done. Let's remember that the idea of leveraging data to solve problems is just as new and uncertain to the customer as it is to the companies serving that customer. Customers need to know whether they've defined the problem properly. Customers further need to understand the possible routes to getting the job done and why your particular offer works better than the next-best alternatives. Customers also need support to look within their own business for other jobs that data and analysis can address, in terms of efficiency, cost savings, or entirely new ways to serve customers. Remember that the idea of TBO is two-sided. It includes the benefits of efficiency and cost savings as well as higher customer revenue through better value creation and value realization.

As a supplier, you also need to know each customer's broader context. Why does this job to be done matter? Can this job be translated into key performance metrics (KPIs)? Which KPI would be most relevant on a customer's dashboard? What might a customer be overlooking? What opportunities can your data, analytics, and insights create for the customer so that they can gain a decisive competitive advantage in their own markets?

In short, successful data monetization requires a robust combination of techno push and market pull. You educate the customer about why you have the best data-driven offer addressing the fundamental goal(s) they pursue (job to be done) and work with them to understand the broader context. This enables you and the customer to identify existing and latent opportunities and to determine how your capabilities can best seize them. That

---

7   Clayton M. Christensen, Scott D. Anthony, Gerald Berstell, and Denise Nitterhouse, "Finding the Right Job for Your Product," *MIT Sloan Management Review,* April 1, 2007.

advantageous combination can only occur through what we call *customer intimacy.*

Turning customer intimacy into value creation

That magnetic bond and relationship tightens and flourishes when it drives the creation of value. The starting point for identifying potential avenues for value creation is exploring and fully understanding your customers' job to be done. This will answer the questions "Where does value lie from our customers' perspective?" and "How can data and analytics contribute to creating that value?"

(main text continues on page 49)

Deep Customer Intimacy to Feed Value Calculators

In 2018 Deloitte Digital developed an online Internet of Things (IoT) / predictive maintenance value calculator to demonstrate the potential return of their 90-day turnkey IoT solution.[1] The use of value calculators is not new in the industrial world. They've been used successfully in IT, in services, and in outsourcing. However, the use of this tool in the field of IoT is quite unique and innovative. Building a credible calculator requires deep customer intimacy about the customer's operations, which includes the following:

1 Customer's scale and scope of operations
2 Customer's operational KPIs
3 Customer's pains and gains translated into numbers
4 Customer's P&L structure understanding

---

1   Extracted from Deloitte's website in May 2018. More information at https://www2.deloitte.com/us/en/pages/operations/articles/iot-roi -calculator.html

Building a credible calculator also requires gathering answers to a series of questions to project a realistic range of benefit quantified in dollars or percentages. These high-level value numbers are used to inform high-level business cases early in the value investigation between suppliers and customers. They serve as a value hook to continue the discussion and eventually conduct a deep analysis of value.

Here are some of the questions:

1 What is the scale of your operations? (very large / large / medium / small)
2 How many production lines do you operate in the factory? (number of lines)
3 What is your production rate (units per hour) for one production line? (number of units)
4 What is the average downtime in a month for one production line? (number of hours)
5 What is the ex-factory price of product (per unit)? ($ figure)
6 What are your factory monthly utility bills (including electricity, water, fuel, oil, gas, etc.)? ($ figure)
7 What is the average number of days that a product spends in inventory before being shipped? (number of days)
8 What is your holding cost per unit of product per day in inventory? ($ figure)
9 What is the average spend on replacement of parts in a factory, per month? ($ figure)
10 On average, how many times a month does production stop because of unscheduled maintenance needs? (number)

Based on these questions, the calculator will quantify some of the typical value drivers of IoT and predictive maintenance such as reduced downtime, increased stock rotation, operational savings, and cash flow optimization due to spare part management. It will then propose a range of ROI based on the provided numbers and some general assumptions. All numbers are for information only!

In the end, the point of this exercise is not to create theoretical formulas for the calculators. It's about having the right KPIs to measure in general or per customer vertical and about having enough customer intimacy to collect the necessary data. These are detailed pieces of information that require relationship, access, and knowledge of the operations. Such information should be collected on an ongoing basis or during customer pilots. Without prior relationships, a production manager might not be willing to share openly the essence of his or her production process.

(continued from page 47)

In this chapter, we show how you can answer that question using a practical job-to-be-done assessment to uncover and understand what B2B customers really want and need in terms of market offers based on data and analytics. We conclude with a discussion of actions that companies must take to ensure that they create revenues and profits through offerings that truly meet customer expectations. This includes organizational changes that foster a culture around data monetization, and steps to achieve what we refer to as *customer intimacy on steroids.*

Turning data into true insights begins with a simple, yet important premise: most B2B customers aren't interested in data itself but in the outcomes that can be derived from data. This means that data has no value in its own right. We've seen many companies that virtually drown in data. They build data warehouses. They diligently add more data each day—to the extent that they actually realize that storing growing amounts of data isn't free; it comes at a substantial cost. But many don't turn data into strategic insights into customer jobs.

In B2B markets, jobs to be done are manifold. They may include reducing maintenance costs on machines or deriving higher productivity from assets invested. To help customers accomplish their goals—to complete these jobs—you need to understand the customer so well that you can define their jobs with precision and find the best data-driven answer to do the job. Instead of the traditional focus on selling features, companies need to dig deeper into what really drives value for customers.

Figure 2.1 illustrates that idea. The top level (customer job to be done) defines the ultimate outcome(s) that customers seek to achieve. Customers typically translate these goals into KPIs monitored on dashboards. The middle level (pains and gains) refers to benefits that customers derive or sacrifices they endure with respect to the nature of the job and the features in the solution. The lowest level refers to the attributes or features bundled into a supplier's offer.

Consider the following example. A major concern of power utilities is avoiding power outages in their grid—by all means. In

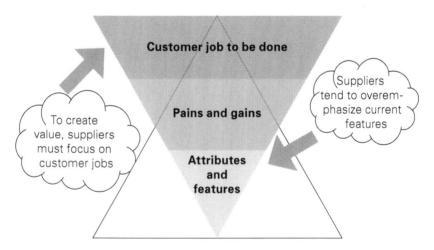

Figure 2.1. The primacy of the *job to be done* as the focus for value creation.

addition to being a major disruption, power outages are extremely costly. One way to address this problem is to reduce the risk of unplanned equipment downtime (i.e., a pain or sacrifice) and to make better use of field technicians' time by having them complete multiple maintenance tasks on one call (i.e., a gain or benefit). How can data and analytics help address these pains and gains? Take the example of an industrial transformer. The transformer can be compared to the blood running through the human body. Much like illness or infections can be detected through blood tests, permanently monitoring oil conditions can raise warning signs for potential equipment failure. If customers can remotely monitor oil in an industrial transformer, the 24/7 data flow from that equipment (i.e., a feature) allows the customer to make decisions—with proper analysis and interpretation—about when to schedule that equipment's next preemptive maintenance. Note that companies often are tempted to work through figure 2.1 from the bottom up: "Here's the data, these are the analyses we can run. How could customers benefit from it?" While this approach is not necessarily wrong, successful data monetization often calls for turning the approach upside down. But this can only be done with deep customer intimacy.

Use laddering to generate deeper customer insights

How to practically gain deeper insights on how to add value through data-driven offers? We've used a technique called *laddering* many times with companies to explore and visualize the linkages between the attributes and features of existing or potential offers, pains and gains perceived by customers, and what the customer ultimately wants, as shown in figure 2.2. You can use laddering to understand whether an existing offer aimed at monetizing data creates sufficient value in the eye of a customer. You

What customers ultimately want to achieve
(job to be done)
Examples: improve asset efficiency,
avoid power outage

What customers perceive as gains and pains
in offer
Examples: reduce machine downtime,
benchmark with competition

What we build into our offer (attributes)
Examples: a data sensor, an algorithm,
a smartphone app

Figure 2.2. How laddering links the phases in the strategic approach to value creation.

can also use laddering to explore how a novel concept or potential new offer could get the customer's job done. Laddering exercises are among the qualitative methods that allow suppliers to gain deeper insights through in-depth interviews with customers.

Let's return to our earlier example of the industrial transformer. This is a relatively commoditized market, where manufacturers permanently seek differentiation. Imagine that one supplier wants to break away from competition by offering a remote monitoring service as a differentiator. You can build ladders from the bottom up to probe whether a service feature really creates value in the eye of the customer. Likewise, you can begin with a customer goal and work your way down. In this case, let's begin by asking customers to explore the new offer and explain which elements are relevant. If possible, have customers compare alternative offers and ask them where they see meaningful differences.

Then you can begin building ladders by asking multiple *why* questions, such as "Why is this important to you?" You typically know you've reached the end of the ladder when the customer can't elicit further ideas in such a chain of consequences, flowing from an existing offer's attributes. Figure 2.3 shows one of several ladders elicited in an hour-long interview.

Laddering can also flow from top to bottom in figure 2.2, that is, by moving down from the job to be done, through the benefits and sacrifices valued by customers, and ultimately establishing a link to the attributes of a potential data-enabled offer. Whether laddering involves existing data offers or new ones, it allows you to drill deeper for insights that can help lay the groundwork for the differentiation, dollarization, and pricing activities we discuss

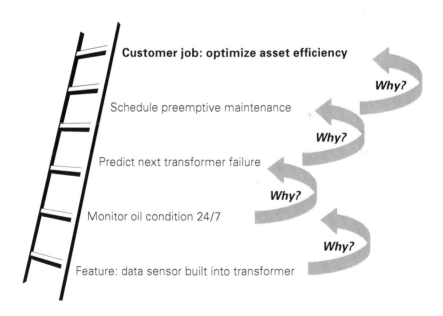

Figure 2.3. Building a ladder from multiple *why* questions (industrial B2B example).

in later chapters. Here's a small sample of the questions that laddering can help answer:

- In what areas is a company's offer the same as the competition's?
- Where is it better or worse?
- Where are new opportunities for monetizing data?
- Where are unmet or unarticulated jobs to be done?
- How can existing data offers be better differentiated?
- What new customer promises can we make tomorrow?
- Which value propositions truly resonate with customers in the data and analytics space?

Customer intimacy requires a 360-degree view of the customer

There's no single path or approach to achieving customer intimacy. A company must examine all available sources to understand how data-enabled services can add value to customers' top and bottom lines. Figure 2.4 is an overview of different data sources that companies can integrate to gain the deepest possible insights for monetizing data. Ideally your approach would be exhaustive, not selective.

Customer intimacy on steroids: Building blocks. Customer intimacy requires a process of turning data into meaningful insights, which in turn serve as a basis for commercial actions, such as redesigning a digital service, modifying a customer promise made, or changing a pricing element. In short, customer intimacy consists of three key building blocks:

$$CI = D \times I \times A$$

(CI = Customer Intimacy; D = Data; I = Insights; A = Actions)

Figure 2.4. Customer intimacy means exhausting all available qualitative and quantitative sources of data.

We present this equation as a multiplication because you can't substitute one element for another. If you're focusing on two elements—say, *data* and *actions*—but missing the third—here, *insights*—then your customer-intimacy outcome is zero. Companies need to work on all three building blocks at the same time.

Role of speed. In addition, several important factors influence the relationships between these Big Three: speed, trust, and endurance. We'll begin with speed. How quickly can a company acquire critical customer data? How quickly can it turn that data into valuable insights? How quickly can it learn and make changes accordingly? Customer intimacy requires new forms of experimentation and quick learning loops to ensure that you bring offers quickly to the market and preempt competition.

Role of trust. A second essential factor impacting customer intimacy—beyond depth and speed—is trust. You can't achieve excellent customer intimacy without a spirit of learning and partnering with customers. Your customers must be on board every step of the way. The most reliable way to gain a customer's buy-in and gain their trust is to show them how they'll profit from giving you data and sharing information with you. Customer intimacy is impossible unless customers open up and share information. This cannot be assumed. As the saying goes, trust must also be earned from customers.

Role of depth. Achieving trust is critical to successfully mastering data monetization. If customers are reluctant to give you access to their information or to share their data and knowledge, the reason is usually simple: they don't trust you! Lack of trust means that customers don't believe that you're a strong data expert or they fear that you won't use data with their best interest in mind. Once you remove this barrier, you'll be able to dig much deeper and to focus on data and insights that allow you to truly move the needle with customers.

We refer to this framework including data, insights, and actions as key building blocks and the enablers speed, trust, and depth as *customer intimacy on steroids*. With this deck of cards in hand (figure 2.5), you can successfully play the data monetization game.

Customer intimacy on steroids, however, is not a goal unto itself. It doesn't matter unless you can take action and translate that intimacy into real-world market offers that create value for customers. We show the three critical steps in figure 2.6. The

Customer intimacy on steroids

- **Re-segmenting** the customer base, including data considerations
- Picking the right **pilot accounts** for a value data initiative
- Mapping the strategic account **footprint**
- Remapping the **buying center** and relevant influence levels
- Building an internal winning **coalition** (around procurement)
- Mapping the customer **operational process**
- Uncovering the stakeholder **pains and gains** with data and digital
- Preparing the **value strategy**: tools, models, dashboards, etc.

Figure 2.5. Some of the steps that constitute customer intimacy on steroids.

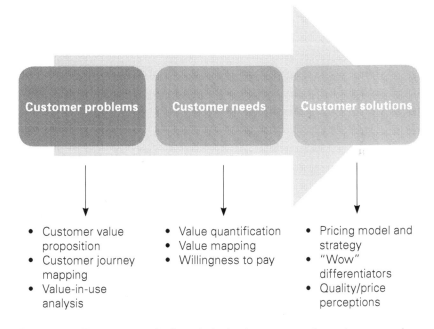

Customer problems	Customer needs	Customer solutions
• Customer value proposition • Customer journey mapping • Value-in-use analysis	• Value quantification • Value mapping • Willingness to pay	• Pricing model and strategy • "Wow" differentiators • Quality/price perceptions

Figure 2.6. The customer is the priority in the process of creating a superior solution.

process begins with accurately defining the customer's problems. The next step involves defining what the customer needs to get critical jobs done and identifying the potential value pool generated if the customer's needs are met. This step includes value quantification, value mapping, and an understanding of what the customer is willing to pay. The final step for the supplier is to determine how its data-driven offer will bring that value to the customer in a way that is superior to the competition. What are the "wow" differentiators? What's the right pricing model for capturing the superior value created?

Role of endurance. Last, we address the matter of endurance. Understanding your customer with the requisite levels of depth, speed, and trust is not a one-off exercise. This needs to become a permanent state of mind, established explicitly within your organization and supported with sufficient resources. Nothing we've described happens organically or automatically. Customer intimacy is a process requiring constant vigilance and conscientious effort. Who within your company is in charge of driving customer intimacy? Who has the capabilities to understand customer processes and combine the qualitative and quantitative investigational tools into one cohesive "machine" for generating customer insights? Running your business around customer intimacy will require different types of experts, different skill sets, and even a different vocabulary. This may well require looking outside your current team for the right people to fill these roles.

Digital innovation begins with customer intimacy. Many of the tools and methods needed in this space are permanent or enduring rather than one-off or spot research and analysis. These in turn place different demands on everyone who interacts with customers. In figure 2.7 we list some of the specific means of generating ongoing customer insights. How prepared are your current internal teams to perform these tasks and nurture these relationships?

> **Digital innovation starts with customer insights**
>
> - Lead user meetings, panels, and councils
> - Customer observations and ethnographic research
> - Customer advisory boards
> - Customer co-creation/experimentation sessions
> - Deep value-in-use analysis
> - Community of enthusiasts and brand evangelists
> - Market and technology radars
> - Signal analysis from near and far industries
> - Customer journey mapping and process blueprinting
> - Brainstorming sessions: day in the life of a customer / staple yourself to an order

Figure 2.7. Specific ongoing tools and methods for generating customer insights.

So, let's say you've set in motion everything we've described. What kinds of projects can you undertake with customers? How fast can you go with them? How many of their internal barriers can you help break down? We highlight a small number of impactful projects in figure 2.8, defining them in terms of the task, the anticipated duration, the stakeholders involved, and the challenges. Not all customers work at the same speed with the same internal processes. You have to help them move along their internal process. Noteworthy is that customer intimacy—as we described it in this chapter—provides the antidote to each of the challenges in figure 2.8. And if customers don't know how to solve these challenges, they need to be able to rely on you to keep going.

Engaging your customer intimately enables you as the supplier to raise your customer's level of digital maturity. Digital innovation is new to them as well. Customers often need a trusted partner who surprises and delights them not only with superior offers but also with more valuable insights into what they (the customer) can do in the market, not just what the partner supplier can do.

Typical customer digital project...

Phases	Business case development	Make-or-buy decision/vendor engagement	Proof of concept	First pilot projects	Rollout and scaling
Duration	3–6 months	1–3 months	3–12 months	6–12 months	6+ months
Stakeholders	Cross-functional team; C-suite involvement	Project team; IT; C-suite sponsor; vendors	Local BU teams; technical teams; vendors	Pilot team; project team; sponsor; vendors	C-suite team; digital champions; vendors; teams
Potential challenge	• Nonrealistic project scope • Short-term approach • Incorrect business KPIs	• Not-invented-here syndrome • Competing internal solutions • Limited technical capabilities	• Lack of alignment • Boil-the-ocean syndrome • No clear vision	• Disruption to core business • Missed $$$ expectations • Delays • Technical issues	• Process changes • Analytics capabilities • Data issues • Time to scale

...customer digital maturity matters!

Figure 2.8. Types of customer projects and their challenges.

Are you already developing those kinds of relationships with your customers? You can bet that if you aren't, one of your competitors will fill the void quickly. If your mission is successful data monetization, the first step in fulfilling that mission is creating and fostering customer intimacy, to establish that unbreakable magnetic bond between you and your customer, between their pull and your push. Customer intimacy is the heart of the matter.

3

Step 1: Map Your Value Constellation

The future of the Industrial Internet will involve partnerships across a variety of players including tech and industrial companies. The key issue: Who will assume the leadership position to extract maximum economic value in such an ecosystem? Will industrial companies take the lead? Or will the digital natives take the lead? Both have a chance.

—*Vijay Govindarajan,*
Harvard Business Review, *February 3, 2018*

IMAGINE THE CHALLENGES AND opportunities that big trucking companies face with respect to data. They manage fleets of up to thousands of vehicles whose service requirements range from engines to fuel to tires to every other part from bumper to bumper. The amount of data generated by these fleets is overwhelming. Because of the opportunities to monetize data and to create customer value within this vast ecosystem, everyone from OEMs (e.g., Volvo) to leasing companies (e.g., Penske) to parts suppliers (e.g., Cummins, Michelin) wants access to the data.

But who will assume the leadership role to turn this data into value for customers? Which companies will put themselves in the best core positions to create and capture value? Nearly every B2B industry today faces these same challenges. Each individual company must ask itself how it wants to monetize data and the extent to which its interests are aligned or misaligned with those of other companies in its own ecosystem.

Answering these and related big-picture questions is what this chapter is about.

The first step for B2B companies is to recognize that they are all part of a broader value constellation with many players who are involved in the data value chain. B2B companies cannot take the myopic view of "me, my equipment, and my data" given what's happening in their digital value constellation. It would hinder efforts to monetize data and potentially do a disservice to customers. They need to understand their current place and role in a value constellation, how that role might evolve over time, and what steps they can take to either defend or leverage their position as the constellation evolves. Who would have thought that Google would work with the US military, that Amazon would become a leader in web services, or that SpaceX would disrupt the space business? A traditional ecosystem analysis would miss the signals that these digital natives or new digital entrants would enter very traditional ecosystems.

The importance of access

In the introduction, we introduced the SAVE framework for understanding how to successfully commercialize data-enabled services. The "A" in that model represents access, which at the highest level means access to customers and access to data. It's hard to imagine a company achieving excellence in customer intimacy when either is lacking. Access creates the degrees of freedom that companies can leverage within their value constellation. Figure 3.1 provides a more nuanced view of access and the steps that a company can take to improve and enhance it.

Anything that weakens access to customers or to data diminishes a company's chances of monetizing data successfully. Conversely, when we dig deeper into what access means, we can derive actions to improve or enhance access in order to benefit the company as well as its customers.

What's a value constellation?

At this point, it's essential to highlight the difference between an ecosystem and a value constellation.

In a business context, an *ecosystem* is a network of interacting organizations, including manufacturers, dealers, service providers, customers, competitors, and government agencies, among

Solution
Access
Value
Education

1 Mapping and leading the value constellation
2 Business modeling through partnerships
3 Building a value stakeholder map
4 Analyzing buying centers

Figure 3.1. Steps to improve and enhance access.

others, involved in (co-)creating goods and services. Actors in a business ecosystem both compete and cooperate with each other.

A *value constellation* is a business ecosystem that identifies and describes how value is created and captured by individual actors in a given business community. This view of value creation departs from the traditional value-chain perspective developed by Michael Porter in the 1980s. According to value-chain logic, individual firms first embed value in their own products and services and then add value in a chain of actors (value stacking) until they reach the final consumer. Note that the Latin root of *consume* means *to eat up, to devour*. So, in a value-chain logic, value is created on one side, a chain of firms, and is eaten up on the other side, by the consumer.

From a value constellation perspective, by contrast, the focus is not on a sequential chain of firms but on the value-creating system itself, within which different parties work together to co-create value.

Value constellations are dynamic. Patterns, connections, and interactions form over time to create unique opportunities despite the potential apparent distance between players. We find that the digital environment is a fast-moving constellation of players across multiple ecosystems all looking to create and capture value. Surprising partnerships and connections are made across the value constellation to accelerate the speed of business. This is why digital transformations are reshaping the traditional view of industrial ecosystems. The injection of massive amounts of data is unleashing impressive opportunities to shape new value constellations. This fundamental change will have a number of consequences. First, well-established players in a market shift from being links in a chain to being like spiders in a web, controlling intersections in a large network. The dynamics of these webs or networks are much different from those in chains, because flows of data and information can easily bypass a company—even an entire sector—that doesn't add as much value as other "spiders" along another path. Existing ties between suppliers, distributors, and customers can be weakened or broken. Aggressive disruptors can forge new positions in value constellations by seizing essential pieces that traditionally belonged to incumbents, who get pushed aside or even eliminated.

But a company can also strengthen existing bonds while creating new ones. What happens depends on its power and position within the value constellation, whose many dimensions are shown in figure 3.2.

You need to know what your value constellation looks like today and identify the forces that will shape its future form tomorrow, two years from now, and five years from now. Where is the vital data coming from, and where is it flowing? Who is collecting, consolidating, and analyzing it? Who is influencing these flows? Once you begin mapping the value constellation, you'll realize that the odds are stacked strongly against a solo play in a traditional ecosystem. Partners and allies are essential. A company can monetize data by guiding others through the value constellation—that is, helping others connect by overcoming information asymmetries. Companies can also monetize the insights from accrued data over time and profit from offering customer insights drawn from pooled, compounded sets of data. Those opportunities, which we elaborate on below, are just three of the many ways a company and its customers can benefit from data monetization.

The value of interconnections

The visibility offered by the Internet can seem like an avalanche or even a tsunami to companies looking to choose a vendor and to vendors looking for customers. Offering a platform that provides a

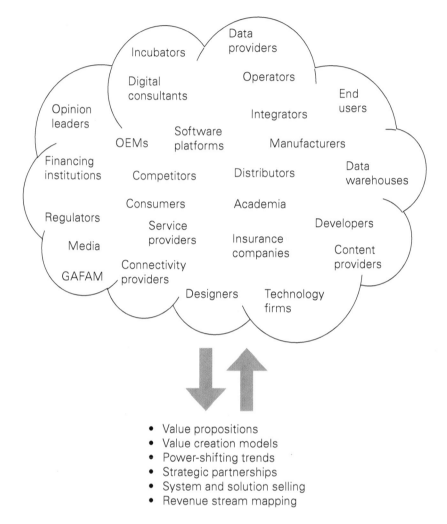

Figure 3.2. The value constellation contains many players with multiple forms and layers of interaction.

matchmaking service can create tremendous efficiency and value by lowering search and customer acquisition costs, reducing risks, and shortening buying and selling cycles. But that role requires a thorough overview of all the potential players in the value constellation. The firm Vixxo performs this role in facility management.

As a platform owner, Vixxo serves as a market maker for large retail chains and the tens of thousands of small, local service providers who provide maintenance, repair work, and other services. Without a platform, such as Vixxo, it would be nearly impossible for either side in these relationships to find the other party efficiently. Such a matchmaker or market maker also provides a central clearinghouse for the supply and demand in this market, which relieves both parties of having to deal with countless systems and people. Finally, the scale and service quality of these platforms create a dependency; switching costs and barriers to entry are high.

(*main text continues on page 72*)

Creating New Value Constellations through Digital Disruption: Vixxo's Three-Sided Platform in Facilities Management

Digital transformation is rapidly reshaping many industries and value constellations among firms. New platform-based business models leveraging data and analytics favor the emergence of new actors in well-established B2B ecosystems and challenge the existence of incumbent players. In the process, yesterday's market leaders often see their traditional power bases and central positions threatened.

For example, in the US, Arizona-based Vixxo disrupted facilities management, a traditional slow-moving industry, with an innovative business model squarely built around data and analytics. Vixxo is a technology-enabled asset management company that provides facility, intelligent energy, and construction management services for clients with geographically dispersed retail portfolios throughout North America.

The company maintains over 1.1 million dispersed revenue-generating critical assets for many Fortune 500 clients in the retail, supermarket, convenience store, and restaurant verticals. Its offers are designed to optimize B2B customers' assets across over 65,000 sites by improving service delivery, reducing costs, and providing strategic insights—all aimed at lowering total cost of ownership.

Established in 2013 through the merger between First Service Networks (FSN) and FM Facility Maintenance (FM), Vixxo today operates 15 services centers across the US and Canada employing more than 1,000 people. With a compound annual growth rate (CAGR) of 37 percent, the company is one of the fastest-growing players in the facilities management industry.

Vixxo disrupted the market by creating a two-sided platform model. The firm serves over 150 Fortune 500 customers with distributed real estate portfolios, leveraging data and analytics to help business customers make better decisions, streamline maintenance, gain visibility into facility investments, and achieve sustained cost savings. Collectively, these customers represent over $1 billion in facility management spend annually.

Vixxo offered a "one-stop shop" solution for over 100 services trades, including electricity; heating, ventilation, and air conditioning (HVAC); lighting; plumbing; refrigeration; and waste management, among many others. The company leverages its expertise to provide asset and facilities management through advanced data analytics, mobility products, and machine-to-machine technologies. Using data on assets, usage, and breakdowns, Vixxo gains unique insights into asset performance, identifies opportunities to achieve cost savings and productivity gains, and works with its clients to ultimately create better in-store experiences for users and end customers.

To achieve the company's mission, the platform connects Vixxo's network of large-scale business customers with a close-knit nationwide network of local service providers to deliver integrated asset management, project, and trade services to clients across the US and Canada. Collectively, these service providers deploy over 150,000 local technicians in addition to Vixxo's own 150 service technicians.

This local provider model translates to savings for business customers, national coverage for multisite facilities, improved asset uptime, and high levels of customer satisfaction. Each provider in Vixxo's network uses Vixxo's proprietary mobile technology platform for consistent data collection on over 1.1 million assets. This data allows Vixxo to gain deep insight to optimize assets and to help its customers make better business decisions. Its technology platform and the granularity of data generated allow Vixxo to effectively differentiate itself from competition in the facilities management industry.

Vixxo's data-driven business model allows the platform operator to standardize and optimize costs of operations nationwide. The model further enables the company to monitor execution performance across service providers, identify opportunities for productivity improvements, and work with service providers. These often are small, privately owned businesses and locally well-established to become a preferred partner. With the help of a well-honed evaluation system, much like a "Yelp for facilities management," service providers are internally ranked on service quality and delivery performance for each single service act performed. The higher a service provider scores in Vixxo's measurement system, the higher it moves up the priority list when bidding for allocation of maintenance and repair business on Vixxo's platform.

Finally, beyond the initial matching of two networks—retail location operators and service providers—Vixxo went one step further to grow its model into a three-sided platform. The company initiated the creation of new ties between retail customers, equipment manufacturers, and itself for unleashing value creation potentials. For example, when working with a global coffeehouse chain, Vixxo identified a small plastic funnel in coffee-brewing machines that often failed because it wasn't designed to endure the coffee temperature it was exposed to. To improve productivity and reduce outage of this strategic asset in coffeehouse stores, Vixxo worked with the machine manufacturer and its store chain customer to replace the part with a solution that prevented thousands of potential disruptions and thus created a better in-store experience.

Clearly, by disrupting a well-established industry and ecosystem of well-established firms, Vixxo unleashed substantial productivity gains and value-creating opportunities. In so doing, Vixxo created new data-driven competitive advantages based on an impressive accumulation of "clean" historical asset-performance data, a superior service provider network, and implementation skills that enable it to execute on a value proposition that deeply resonates with business customers.

(*continued from page 69*)

The value of accrued data

One of the most enlightening aha moments in data monetization occurs when a company realizes the vast but hidden value in data that has accrued over time. Most companies focus so intensely on real-time data that they overlook the immense potential value of accumulated historical data. Controlling such a data set confers an unbeatable competitive advantage, because replicating the data is impossible, and approximating it gets harder the more extensive the data is.

We recount the story of a Fortune 500 manufacturer that developed a software application to run together with its installed equipment. The development team realized that the app would give it access to and make visible the performance of their machines—and other interconnected machines—across dozens of data parameters. They would be the only spider at that spot in the web, so to speak, and the data they'd collect would allow them to define context-specific performance benchmarks and best practices for every industry their equipment operated in. In terms of jobs to be done, such a company can use its data and insights to help optimize an entire industry, creating even more value for its partners and their customers.

The value of combined, compounded data

A manufacturer may be tempted to say "I want to keep MY data" and "I'm not going to let anyone else have or use MY data." Proprietary data does have value, but questions remain: Within the given value constellation, which company is best placed to not only access data but also monetize it? Which company can make itself indispensable in the data value chain? And can you be that company?

Think of it this way: imagine that one company collects only verbs, one collects only nouns, and one collects punctuation marks. When customers value *sentences* and ultimately *ideas,* these companies will have to find a way to work together. The power of their data—its power to generate valuable insights—is compounded when combined with other data sources. Data that is precious and proprietary may make much more sense in combination with data or context provided by others within the value constellation. This is the essence of what we mean by mapping and, if possible, leading the value constellation. That map helps a company look beyond its own horizons and gain new insights. The growing interest in digital consulting services related to benchmarking performance across actors (e.g., workflow optimization based on medical scanner throughput across hospitals) illustrates the growing role of compounded data.

Long live manufacturing!

It may seem strange to make this comment in a book on data monetization. But when everyone in a market chases the golden ring of data monetization, many will fall short. That's simple math. As value constellations evolve, some companies may be best served by riding a pendulum swing from services back to products.

In a B2B value constellation, there will be winners and losers with respect to data monetization. Some winners will find faster and better ways to become the spider in the web that customers and partners depend on. The alternative for others could be to camp on their positions, stay superior in product expertise, and accept their role as product and data purveyors for others. That might be their only viable option. It may be better to be a product supplier in someone else's value equation than to close down your factories or continue pouring effort into the lost cause of competing against a better spider.

In many cases this is also a question of talent and culture. Visit many B2B companies today, tap any person on the shoulder, and ask them if the company is good at developing, manufacturing, and selling its products. Many people will say, "Of course." But when you ask them how good their company is at monetizing data, you may get a puzzled expression.

In the end, successful data monetization means finding your best spot in your ever-changing value constellation. You have to be realistic about what resources and capabilities you have, what resources and skills you'll have to acquire, and make the best of it.

Understanding and leveraging the sources of data

Data can be created in so many ways, as we show in figure 3.3. But the critical question is the location of critical data within the value constellation, along with the "control" questions: who owns

Build your value constellation: where is the data you need?

Core data	Supplemental data
• Asset sensor data • Product sensor data • Production data • Operational data • Maintenance data • Health and usage data • Product quality data • Work/repair order data **Think of ownership, access, control, rights, security**	• Environmental factors • Utility data • Procured product data • Supply/demand forecast data • Warranty data • Customer service data • Social media data • Consumer usage data • General CRM data • Commercial transaction data • Technical support data

Figure 3.3. Where is the data you need?

the data, who has access to it, and who is authorized to access and use it. Figure 3.3 shows how broad and complex different types of data are and reinforces two key points in this chapter: it often requires additional data to unlock the full value of a data set, and the company best positioned to monetize the data is not always the owner of the data.

Many data-enabled initiatives struggle because the company has not fully visualized the value constellation for commercializing its data or found a position within that network so that data can directly or indirectly generate the greatest value for customers. Data quality matters as well. Have potential partners identified the right data and aggregated it correctly? Who has developed the "clean" data that can be analyzed and put into a commercial package? Are the data speaking the same language in the end? Within any value constellation you'll find smaller networks and even chains along which value is created. The company needs to make these steps visible, understand the access rights, and identify partner capabilities needed at each step.

Finding the right partners

One of the implications of access, as we showed in figure 3.1, is the opportunity to create new business models with partners. When several companies connect to get the greatest value out of their collective data, it's natural to expect a power shift from one firm to another, due either to capabilities, to customer relationships, or to the isolated value of the data that an individual company brings to the table. When you look at value constellations, different combinations of companies can create similar offers in parallel because they have different and sometimes complementary data that can solve the same job to be done from a different angle.

This is a caveat for companies pursuing data monetization. You have to know what potential competitors and partners are doing because there are multiple paths to success and multiple paths to failure in a value constellation. The risk is particularly acute in traditional B2B markets or value constellations where established players have created a niche for themselves with premium prices on products, equipment, or machines. But the risk is even greater when digital natives are entering traditional B2B ecosystems with speed, agility, and technical expertise. An inability to monetize data-enabled services may erode their margins and relegate the company to secondary status within the value constellation.

Based on the famous business model canvas developed by Osterwalder and Pigneur,[8] figure 3.4 shows the critical elements related to partnerships when rethinking your data monetization business model. The right combination of partners and customers increases a company's ability to innovate by infusing fresh perspectives, enabling co-creation of value, and expanding the pool of customers to pilot with and scale to.

---

8   Alexander Osterwalder and Yves Pigneur, *Business Model Generation: A Handbook for Visionaries, Game Changers, and Challengers* (Hoboken, NJ: Wiley, 2010).

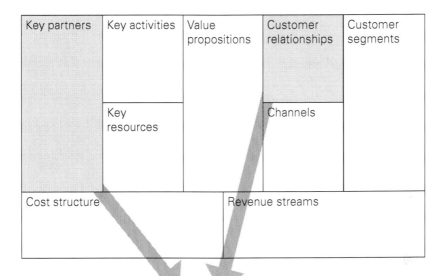

1   Open innovation
2   Partnership strategy for business development
3   Value co-creation and value sharing
4   Co-incubation of customer pilot projects

Figure 3.4. Business modeling through partnerships. Adapted, with permission, from Strategyzer.com.

How can these companies actually work with each other? Who will assume the leading role in the web? These questions have no easy answers. Companies need a full 360-degree view of their market because they will need to play offense and defense at the same time. While an experienced incumbent might be looking to monetize its historical data, a disruptive competitor may be using artificial intelligence (AI) or machine learning to develop comparable expertise that is sufficient to displace that incumbent—in a very short time. In the digital space, first-mover advantage holds true. If there's one key partnership to make and you're late, one of your competitors might make the move before you. So what's the plan B to get the data or the required technology?

This is a 21st-century version of the outcome of disruption in many industries over the last several decades. Disruptors with a different and ultimately better understanding of customer value have fundamentally altered industries ranging from cars to airlines to retail to consumer electronics. History has shown what happens when companies don't buy in to these transformations, appreciate them, and figure how to embrace them. Those who don't really do disappear. It's game over. The corporate graveyards are filled with former stars that crashed hard and fast. There's no reason to believe that the world of data monetization will be immune to that outcome. So go out and hack your own business before somebody else does. Can you mutate yourself enough to remain competitive? Shed traditional value-chain analyses and embark on mapping your value constellation to profit from data monetization.

4

Step 2: Revisit Your Customer Segmentation

Companies will want to focus on their most progressive customers. Traditional customers are important, of course, but they are less likely to come up with fresh ideas that lead to real innovation. Instead, companies should look for inspiration and input from exciting new players, whose mindset is more likely to be shaped by the possibilities of the latest technology and digital transformation. . . . Again, close co-development with customers will be extremely helpful. Indeed, successful companies often find that their customers in many ways turn out to be the best product managers.

—*"Mastering the Industrial Internet of Things (IIoT),"*
Roland Berger Focus, *September 2017*

ASK MANAGERS IN INDUSTRIAL companies about their customer segmentation for data-enabled services, and they are liable to say, "I already have a customer segmentation. Why don't I just use that?"

It's true that the segmentation you used for years to sell products and hardware may overlap somewhat with the segmentation you'll need for data-enabled services. But how strong is that overlap, and what could you be missing? When companies grow beyond products into services and customer solutions, managers often find that they need a different segmentation scheme to fully tap the potential of services revenues and profits. The same logic applies to data-driven offers. Remember: data-enabled offers are more and more synonymous with services. The brief story below illustrates the importance of challenging and adjusting your existing segmentation.

Think about how an ATM manufacturer might sell its equipment to financial institutions. ATMs must meet greatly varying technical specifications: transaction times, customer interface and display quality, capacity and accessibility, physical security and durability, and integration into a bank's IT infrastructure. Within the traditional tender process, sales conversations revolve largely around product features. Which ATM performs better than the competition on technical characteristics and purchasing requirements? As a result, the manufacturer will have a segmentation in place that classifies banks by criteria such as geography, types and volumes of machines bought, and perhaps willingness to pay.

Fast forward 10 years to 2018 and beyond, and the ATM has evolved from its original role as a cash dispenser (the acronym stands for "automated teller machine") into a node in a bank's data network. To some customers, the ATM is now part of their overall approach to customer relationship management (CRM). Others view the ATM as a lever for driving down the costs of money flowing in, through, and out of the local branch. The machine's ability to interact with customers, collect customer data, and display commercial offers positions it well to become an important part of marketing efforts. As an ATM manufacturer, your sale now also becomes a conversation about how your equipment contributes to your customer's CRM strategy, and new customer stakeholders, such as a bank's marketing director, join the negotiations. How would that change your segmentation?

This chapter explores the need for a B2B company to review and potentially revise its customer segmentation as it transitions from selling hardware to selling data-enabled services and solutions. We're not suggesting that you reflexively throw away your existing segmentation. You've invested a lot of hard work, empirical evidence, and knowledge in it, and it may still be a valuable tool for equipment sales. We're recommending that you make sure you have a dedicated segmentation for data-enabled services and solutions that helps you identify the best opportunities and capitalize on them. As you can imagine, doing this upfront as part of the development of your data-enabled offer is paramount, as it impacts the rest of your opportunity framing. In fact, it's the logical next step after mapping your value constellation. You might have to conduct several segmentation exercises with different stakeholders in your value constellation (OEMs vs. end users vs. integrators, for example). The reason for that is that your digital partnership map has expanded and you need to understand what players to select to enable your business model.

How data-enabled solutions and digital markets impact segmentation

The classic approach to segmentation is to group customers with similar characteristics and behaviors into one bucket while recognizing marked differences between buckets. The power shift in the nature of the sale—from product to data-enabled solution— means that you might need to reclassify your customers using different criteria. The challenge is twofold, as figure 4.1 visualizes. The first challenge is that your company has an immutable structure. You still have to continue to operate in plants, legal entities, and regions. The emergence of new, complex, data-enabled offerings adds a twist to this dimension, as some of the offerings' components might come from different units within your company and from outside. The second challenge is the need to revisit your horizontal axis, which is mostly related to go-to-market strategies, including your digital programs. This includes taking a fresh look at buying centers, revisiting relationship maps, and

Figure 4.1. The hybrid segmentation has two dimensions (internal and external).

understanding the buying criteria for data-enabled offers. This is where most of the focus should be, and it's not business as usual!

Recall the ATM scenario. You're now selling a complex solution, not a piece of hardware. The nature of the sale and the conversation are different, which means you'll no longer be talking only to the usual suspects at a potential customer. Of course you'll still meet with purchasing and with the IT teams who integrate the hardware. But because this ATM is now a tool for operational optimization, you'll also speak with general management. Because it's a fraud prevention tool, you may speak with security and risk management. Because it's a potential marketing and CRM tool, you'll speak with the institution's marketing, advertising, and sales teams. Who are these people, and what do they want from your data-rich offering? Why should they spend an hour listening to you? Most importantly, what will you tell them?

When your sales team needs to move beyond the usual suspects, they leave their comfort zone and need to establish entirely new contacts. The better the playbook you give them, the more confident and effective they'll be in building these new coalitions. The basis for the playbook is your customer segmentation for data-enabled services. Figure 4.2 summarizes the changes that will force you to revisit your existing segmentation.

Impact of digital on customer segmentation

- Shift of power in the value constellation and ecosystem
- New customer classification criteria for clustering
- New entire segment or new subsegments
- New buying center analysis
- New critical stakeholders to identify and access

Figure 4.2. The fundamental changes when your sales conversation shifts from hardware to data-enabled solutions.

Let's focus now on the new criteria for customer segmentation. Remember, the world of data-enabled services is new territory for your customers as well. They're learning rapidly, trying to carve out their own advantages. This leads to the first of several criteria, as we elaborate below.

- **Digital maturity.** How well have customers themselves adjusted to digital transformations? Do they "speak" the same digital language? Do they actively ask for your data-driven offers to help them make productivity gains? Do you have to push them? You can grade them as low, medium, or high.
- **Digital culture.** Have they launched their own successful services in the market? Do they leverage digitization internally for process improvements? Are they struggling? Do they have business units, job titles, and executive and operational functions built around digital? You can grade them along the classic adoption cycle: pioneers, early adopters, late adopters, and laggards.
- **Data readiness profile.** Do they have the infrastructure to support data-enabled services? That is a fancy way of asking whether they know how to collect, clean, interpret, and analyze data for commercial purposes. Do they make decisions based on data? You can grade them as basic, intermediate, or advanced.
- **Digital partnership approach.** In chapter 3 we stressed that success in a value constellation depends on the quality of your partners. Do they have a formal process in place for selecting, integrating, and working with partners?
- **Digital prestige.** Do you hear their name mentioned positively and often in conversations? What's their media footprint and reputation? You can grade them as low, medium, or high.

- **Digital investments.** Review their press reports and public filings. How much have they invested in digital, both in absolute terms and in share of investment? How much are they going to invest next? You can grade them as low, medium, or high.
- **Digital sense of urgency.** Do they want your solution yesterday? How demanding are they? Or do they come across as overly cautious, risk averse, and slow to move? You can grade them as low, medium, or high.
- **Internal change agent.** Can you identify these people? Who is leading the digital initiative? This could be any C-level executive, but who they are (CIO, CDO, CMO, CFO, CEO) will say something about their goals and their seriousness. To what extent is the C-suite clearly driving the process? You can grade them as low, medium, or high.

Now you can appreciate why your digital offers might require a different segmentation scheme. If one of the established key accounts in your current segmentation is still in the Stone Age regarding digital offers, what do you do? If they don't get the message, lack the maturity, can't speak about data, and don't intuitively grasp the ROI from data-enabled services, they won't be interested right now. The level of hand-holding required to get them interested will be intense. These customers are not the low-hanging fruit. Focusing on customers like that—no matter how strong the traditional relationship is—could be an egregious misallocation of your resources when building the market for your data-enabled services. Your new segmentation must expose variance across customer contexts and needs like these and offer your marketing and sales teams guidance for prioritizing customers. That raises the following question: do you have the required knowledge about your current customers and prospects on these new digital classification criteria? Don't underestimate the task. Finding out about culture, data maturity, and IT philosophy will require some digging.

The role of a dedicated digital segment

What we said in the previous section does not necessarily invalidate your existing segmentation. That key account we called out still represents an important share of your business, and you can't dismiss that. Revisiting your digital segmentation doesn't mean that these large important customers get downgraded or kicked out. An important customer account may well fall into one segment for equipment sales but be part of a different segment for new digital offers. They keep their key account managers and special treatment, but they are clearly a lower priority for digital. The need to live in both worlds at the same time is another reason why you need to revisit your existing segmentation and understand what you can keep and where you need to adjust or add.

(main text continues on page 89)

Re-segmenting for Digital Disruption, *by Thales InFlyt Experience*

In a February 8, 2018, interview with *Business Insider*, Emirates Airline president Sir Tim Clark issued a dire message to the airline industry about the need to embrace the seismic shift in technology that's under way:

> Guys, there's a storm coming, and if you don't get on it and deal with it, you will perish. The company of the 2050s will bear no resemblance to the company of 2018.... It's not a question about using advanced

technology to increase the way you do your business, like ancillary revenue streams, because that's a given. It's not a question of not knocking your companies down internally and rebuilding them on digital platforms. That's a given for us. It's not the case for a lot [of other airlines].

All airlines are undergoing some phase of digital transformation regardless of the traditional segment they're in. Here are some of the trends we're seeing:

- Many airlines have begun to organize independent digital departments. They recognize that airlines might become e-commerce platforms in the air!
- They understand the power of e-enabled aircraft and big data but don't know how yet to exploit the opportunities.
- Airlines have plenty of data, but it's in silos and very hard to connect and integrate.
- They're looking for help from outside: Etihad Airways signs a USD 700 million technology services cloud collaboration agreement with IBM; Air France–KLM plans to invest more than €200 million in digital and data development by 2020; Emirates is working with five of Oxford University's departments to help analyze its passenger data in order to create new services and operational advantages; and JetBlue has taken space in Silicon Valley to invest in travel startups with the intention of incorporating innovation back into the airline.

This digital tsunami forces marketing organizations to rethink their customer interactions, refresh their customer segmentation, and redesign their go-to-market approaches. Traditional segmentation analysis using solely buying behavior for traditional hardware and software solutions is not enough. For example, airlines traditionally are segmented into low-cost carriers, traditional carriers, and luxury carriers. For these segments, suppliers traditionally sell using a good/better/best approach focusing on hardware, entertainment solutions, and services. Many suppliers avoid the low-cost airlines, as they are often considered price buyers. Digital has changed the game. You could surely propose state-of-the-art, data-driven solutions to a low-cost airline that seeks to generate ancillary revenues. They might need affordable hardware to make this happen. That becomes a trigger. At the same time, luxury airlines might still be interested in upscale passenger experience not using traditional hardware or using a more advanced product. Digital is a game changer in the commercial aviation landscape.

We propose the following steps to refreshing your traditional customer segmentation:

1 Revisit your customer segmentation process by adding digital- and data-classification criteria.
2 Identify new customer segments and/or reclassify your existing segments based on current and newly added classification criteria. You might consider hybrid segmentation as well.
3 Identify new stakeholders within the airlines that have traditionally had little interest in your solutions. Examples are representatives of customer analytics, market intelligence, passenger experience, brand strategy, IT, and digital transformation departments.
4 Map your digital ecosystem to find out who might partner with you to address the needs of new segments. Include these new partners in your business model canvas.
5 Align your marketing, account management, and experience team with the new digital needs of your segments. There are tremendous opportunities in e-commerce, entertainment, and advertising.

> The world of commercial airlines has changed forever if you believe the latest trends and the words of Sir Tim Clark. And the speed of change is accelerating as more digital investments are made and airlines realize the value of data. Our company, Thales InFlyt Experience, is morphing from a hardware- or product-centric company to a provider of personalized entertainment solutions powered by big data and our unique access to the Thales artificial intelligence technology. This is an opportunity to partner with new and innovative companies in the areas of advertising, e-commerce, media content, and data analytics.

(*continued from page 69*)

From a practical standpoint, the most expedient solution to the segmentation question includes the options shown in figure 4.3. You could maintain large existing segmentations and supplement them with a digital segment in parallel. Or you may find that your existing segmentation makes no sense in a digital world, meaning you need to create what we call a *transverse digital segment* that cuts across your existing segments.

Think about Segment 1 in figure 4.3. They may all buy the same products the same way, as before. But for services, some customers may need a lot of hand-holding, tutoring, and training, while others may need no additional consulting or training. In terms of the new digital criteria, the latter customers have the maturity and urgency, speak the language, and have an infrastructure in place to integrate an important new partner. Of course that affects how you'd prioritize customers! So we're essentially asking whether the fundamental distinctions you've historically made between segments still hold when we talk about data-enabled offers.

This discussion about segmentation is not just relevant for the framing of a data-enabled offer. It's an existential discussion that marketing teams need to have in the core business. When it

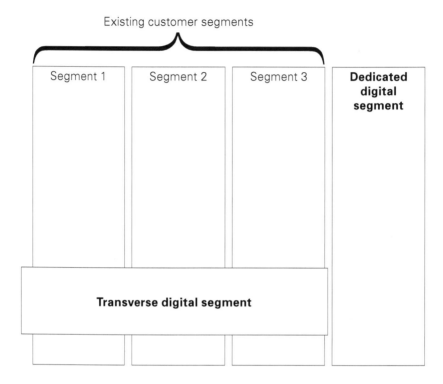

Figure 4.3. Do you need a dedicated digital segment, or does your digital segmentation need to cut across your existing one?

comes to segmentation, there is no "digital" versus "traditional" business. There are customers! So the customer segmentation discussion needs to happen in the business units and must include this new digital dimension.

Making new friends at the customer

The digital conversation is different not only in its purpose and content but also in who is talking and listening. Within the customer you'll have to identify or prioritize new stakeholders.

In this different context, who is now the user, the buyer, or the payer? Who is a gatekeeper? Each of these stakeholders, and their respective roles, will require a different message and potentially will want to see different elements of your digital offers. Who will become your advocate? Who will help sell your offer inside? These individuals, these new friends you need to make, have different needs, experience, budgets, and buying criteria and operate under different soft and hard incentive systems. That's why it's not sufficient to understand the customer from the corporate or aggregated level and how those market needs are changing. You also need to understand how that customer's internal processes have changed. Figure 4.4 illustrates these new coalitions who either are part of the core buying center or operate independently as important stakeholders.

Have you identified the critical stakeholders for your data-enabled offers? Has the composition of the buying center changed? In other words, have some of the new parties (dark circles) in figure 4.4 earned a permanent seat at the table? How do these shifts change each party's weight and influence in the purchase decision? At the simplest level you're trying to understand who they are, why they're involved, and their relative importance in the buying decision. In the digital world, new functions are playing a key role in the digital buying center. Let's take an example. Suppose you're selling an IIoT solution to a pulp and paper manufacturer. Of course you'll have to meet with manufacturing, maintenance, and supply-chain functions to discuss the business side of the data-enabled opportunity. But you'll also need to think about embedding your solution in the overall infrastructure. You'll need to access the control and power rooms in the facilities and install equipment in them. You'll have for sure advanced discussions with the data- and IT-related functions. The stakeholder map and buying center have expanded. More functions have a

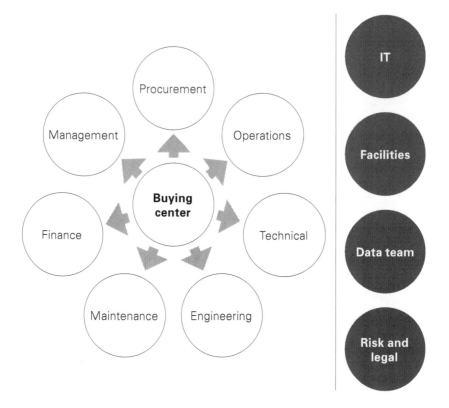

Figure 4.4. Stakeholder mapping: Who participates in the buying center?

role to play and potential weight in the decision to invest or not. The first challenge is identifying these new players and getting to know them. No one will give you access to their assets the first time you meet with them!

Rethinking your sales teams

The answers to these questions may change who participates in the selling center on your side. Will you use parallel salesforces? Will you have salespersons dedicated to selling data-driven offers, while others continue to focus on your "traditional" goods and services? Will you name highly specialized experts supporting generalist salespersons on an as-needed basis? How will you incentivize your sales reps? Let's assume your company follows the 80/20 rule, meaning that 20 percent of your customers represent the bulk of your business. Will that still apply for data-enabled services? Do you treat them separately as their share of your revenue grows, or do you reward your sales teams on overall revenue or on their current metrics? If they have a profit-based incentive and data-enabled services prove much more profitable than hardware sales, how do you compensate the key account manager who still calls on the high-volume account with low digital maturity? Inversely, if selling data-driven services appears to be complex and time-consuming, and if incentives are not aligned, your salespeople will vote with their wallet and stay put. Remember, salespeople are a crowd. Without their buy-in for selling digital offers, your ambitious initiative won't gain traction. Wolfgang has published his findings from working with executives on steering the transition from a product-centric to a service-savvy salesforce.[9] The factors key to mastering this transformation identified are also relevant to selling complex data-driven offers in B2B. Your new segmentation will serve as an important input for resolving these issues, retaining objectivity, and keeping your own sales teams engaged and on board.

How do you prioritize your own services?

This is another critical area where a segmentation for data-enabled services is beneficial. It will help you understand what the demand

---

9   Wolfgang Ulaga and James Loveland, "Transitioning from Product to Service-Led Growth in Manufacturing Firms: Emergent Challenges in Selecting and Managing the Industrial Sales Force," *Industrial Marketing Management* 43 (January 2014): 113–25.

looks like in your market, both now and in the future, depending on how you want to allocate your resources. The end-use combinations you can sell will depend strongly on the size and willingness to pay of the digitally savvy customers. That means you need to prioritize your end uses, as we show in figure 4.5.

This process is a rating model along a small set of powerful criteria. Look at end use 3. This takes the best advantage of your existing assets, would theoretically have a high impact in the market, and even performs best on your additional subjective criteria N. But your customers do not (yet) see the value of that solution. In contrast, end use 1 looks like the most lucrative and impactful solution but the one you are least prepared to offer now. Where do you put your resources? We can't answer that question for you or even offer an empirical rule of thumb. Our point, though, is the point of this chapter. Give yourself the best possible basis for making those kinds of decisions. You need to

- identify the new buying and selling criteria for your data-enabled solutions
- re-evaluate your customers along those criteria
- determine how well those results correspond to your existing segmentation and what changes are necessary

End uses	High value	High impact	Leveraging current assets	Criteria N	
End use 1	++	+++	−	+	Top 5 priority end-use targets
End use 2	+	+	+	=	
End use 3	−	++	+++	+	
End use N	−−	+	++	=	

Figure 4.5. What do we sell and prioritize? That depends on value. What do your customers (based on your new segmentation) want, what do they need, and what are they willing to pay for?

- identify and get to know the digital stakeholders on the customer side, as the conversation shifts from the usual suspects to new friends
- prioritize customers as well as the end uses you can offer.

Remaining focused is essential in the digital world. You should focus on a few customers, a few critical end-use applications, and a couple of customer segments. Chasing all opportunities across all segments and geographies is a mistake that many B2B companies make at the beginning of their digital journey. The lack of focus might have you chasing the wrong opportunities with the wrong customers. This is a philosophical change that GE Digital has made and that others have copied over the past years. GE Digital now focuses their digital efforts in three verticals closely aligned with their core business: aviation, health care, and power. Deloitte Digital learned from this change and also proposes a very focused approach in the early stage of the transformation.

Communicating internally that you need a new segmentation may be greeted with eye-rolls or even outright resistance. But we feel that the case we've laid out in this chapter will appeal to the self-interest at all levels of your organization. It's like returning to a city you haven't visited in years. Better to be prepared with a new map of the customer landscape, driven by an up-to-date GPS, than to rely entirely on your old paper map and your experience. It's definitely not business as usual!

5

Step 3: Select the Right Pilot Customers

Executives don't need to spend months to devise and launch a massive program. Instead, they should seek to identify and prioritize specific use cases that can deliver quick wins. We have seen that good cases to start with take as little as 10 to 12 weeks to turn around, on average.

—Kim Baroudy, Pallav Jain, Sunil Kishore, and Sumesh Nair, "Maximizing Value from Advanced Analytics in Telco Service Operations," McKinsey & Company, January 2018

SO FAR THE FIRST two steps of the Data Monetization Roadmap have given you solid direction. By mapping your value constellation and revisiting your customer segmentation, you've gained the strategic customer insights you need. You know where value lies for your customers, how power is distributed within the value constellation, and what motivates the important stakeholders. Because you're armed with your preliminary value analysis or with data you collected when deploying your prototype offer internally, your logical next step is to seek external validation, which means setting up and implementing your customer pilots. From working with firms on data monetization, we've come to understand that the sooner you do your homework and develop your own pilot projects, and the sooner you involve one or more key customers in developing and validating your digital offer together, the greater your chances of success and your ability to accelerate the process of scaling up your offer.

Setting up and conducting customer pilots may seem straightforward. But in the world of monetizing data, it's not business as usual. Companies must be extra careful when they design their testing and validation strategy because of the following considerations:

1 Digital offers are new for everyone, including customers, even though some of the main players have been working at it for a decade or so.
2 Most value propositions are based on unproven assumptions; further validation is needed.
3 While many firms are quick to make bold claims, we've seen few compelling success stories so far.

The reality is that there are a lot of misconceptions and challenging questions. Implementing a pilot project in cooperation with a customer to reach a proof of concept, fine-tune the offering, and settle all open questions related to commercializing is different from piloting traditional products or services. Companies can't select their customer target based on convenience or on "I have access; therefore, it's a good target." In our experience, this is too often how customers are selected for very complex projects. You can imagine that doing a pilot with the wrong customer might not lead to the ideal outcome.

Other pressing questions about customer pilots are whom you should pilot with, how to select pilot customers, how long pilot projects should last, how to convince the customer to pilot with you and you only, and who at your company will lead the effort. This is not a time for improvisation or guesswork. Answering these questions requires a structured strategic process.

(main text continues on page 101)

Piloting Digital Offers with Customers: Signify and Carrefour Partner for Smart Lighting in France, *by Juliette K. Ulaga, Signify*

Today, many companies transition from manufacturing products to providing services and customer solutions. Consider the example of Signify, previously known as Philips Lighting. In the service arena, the tech giant's former lighting division focuses on three key service domains: Professional, Lifecycle, and Managed Services. In these areas, Signify develops its position as a global leader across Europe, Latin America, North America, and Asia Pacific by growing its portfolio of services that unlock business value in innovative ways.

The world leader in lighting products, systems, and services develops data-enabled services by leveraging the Internet of Things (IoT) to transform homes, buildings, and urban spaces. Smart Street Lighting, also referred to as Connected Lighting, is a good example of a data-enabled service; it allows a city's public light points to be collected and shared through onboard intelligence and integrated sensors. Another example of Smart Street Lighting is dimming lights automatically when streets are empty and increasing brightness when motion is detected, to prevent accidents. In the corporate world, the Wayfinding system is used in a building equipped with a connected lighting system to facilitate mundane tasks. For example, Signify's Wayfinding system can be used to flash a meeting room's lights to signal to employees that a meeting is almost over. Similarly, the system can track and deliver data to indicate that certain office spaces are underused, to help employees find available desks and meeting rooms. But Connected Lighting services also reach way beyond lighting. For example, sensors can greatly benefit law enforcement by helping authorities pinpoint exactly where gunshots have been fired.

One of the ways that Signify launches new data-driven services is through partnering with customers. For example, the company recently developed a pilot project with Carrefour, the world's third-largest retailer, to co-incubate a GPS-style indoor positioning technology that uses LED lights. The retail giant's store based in Lille, France, is the first in the world to use the new LED lighting technology. Philips installed 2.5 kilometers of energy-efficient LED lighting within the 8,000-square-meter store.

Carrefour benefits from the technology in many ways, such as through improved store lighting and reduced energy costs. LED lighting can also serve as a location platform. LED lights flicker at a very high frequency undetectable to the human eye but visible to a smartphone's camera. The position of the lights enables exact tracking of the position of the smartphone. Carrefour has developed a user-friendly app for customers to use while shopping in the store to localize their products. This pilot app currently locates promotional products only, but Signify and Carrefour seek to expand its scope to include the full store inventory. Eric Rondolat, Signify's chief executive officer, states that "it is the most accurate indoor positioning system that exists. Another advantage is that you do not need to develop a parallel infrastructure. You use an existing infrastructure, which at the same time is also providing energy efficiency."

Marie-France Crevecoeur, Signify's business leader of services, highlights three main pieces of advice that companies should consider when deciding whether and how to grow their data-enabled services portfolio. First, they should ask, "Who owns the data?" Crevecoeur explains: "It's a myth to believe that the company or person processing the data is also the one owning the data. On the contrary, it's the end user who owns the data." The second piece of advice is that the legal framework around data privacy, specifically in Europe, reaches deep into the combination of "location, people, and information."

"The key strategy," she reveals, "is to play with the data to anonymize it by using the numbers without revealing the reference to individual people." The third piece of advice is "rather than building all the applications yourself, you must look into the ecosystem and identify wisely the partner with whom you wish to collaborate in the mid- to long term."

In conclusion, Crevecoeur urges companies to plan ahead by defining the value upfront, testing the value with the customer, and defining in which ecosystem the company will decide to position itself to obtain valuable results that will create the most value for the customer and for Signify.

(*continued from page 99*)

Whom to pilot with ... and how to choose them

Your sales team has the most intensive contact with your customers. So it would seem natural to begin the piloting process by asking them for appropriate candidates. The problem is that the sales team will have no shortage of recommendations, but they will apply an insufficient or incomplete set of criteria. You're likely to receive too many suggestions of convenience, meaning that the salespeople will suggest candidates for whom access is easiest or sales activity is strongest. To identify the right candidates, you need a process with clearly defined criteria and a scoring system. Our recommended criteria are summarized in figure 5.1.

These criteria reflect the key issues we raised earlier about customer intimacy, value constellation, and segmentation. This means that you should have already done enough homework to evaluate your customers quickly and accurately according to these criteria.

- **Relationship.** How tight is the bond between you and that customer? How strong is their interest in working with you on digital transformation? It's a good sign if customers are already

Criteria for selecting data pilot customers

- Customer's established relationship with your digital team
- Declared sense of urgency in a digital transformation
- Digital maturity level (medium to high)
- Caliber of the customer's digital sponsor (CEO, CDO, CMO)
- Documented investments in a digital platform
- Propensity to partner with suppliers
- Value-buying behavior in their existing core business
- Risk of core business being disrupted (high)
- Clear and identified customer problem
- Implementation risk and complexity
- Access to relevant stakeholders in the buying center
- Transferability of the pilot work to other customers in the segment

Figure 5.1. The selection of pilot customers should follow a process with strict criteria.

addressing their own digital challenges, are reflecting on their approach to digitization, and have done preliminary homework with you and your team.

- **Urgency.** To what extent have they expressed a sense of urgency? Beyond what your digital team has heard or observed, you can review press reports, public filings, or other declarations of intent. The greater the urgency, the greater the likelihood that they'll move fast and with purpose in a pilot.

- **Digital maturity.** We defined digital maturity in chapter 4. You want to focus on customers with a medium to high level of maturity. We elaborate on this later in this chapter.

- **Sponsor.** What organizational rank does the potential sponsor of a pilot project hold? The concern is that the pilot may not receive the proper commitment, attention, or resources without a champion within the customer organization who can make decisions and mobilize resources quickly.

- **Investments.** Does the pilot candidate have an appetite for and a history of making digital investments?

- **Value buyer.** The term *value buyer* does not mean *price buyer.* Here we literally mean a customer interested in gaining more value from working with you: in other words, one who'll look at alternative technologies that can improve the customer business, then seek out and expect a higher level of performance from suppliers.

- **Disruption risk.** How "dangerous" or disruptive could the results of the pilot be? You don't want to scare off a potential valid customer, but having a large number of "safe" pilots with too-incremental changes ultimately does neither you nor your customers any good.

- **Clear problem definition.** Does the customer know what they want? Have they clearly identified and articulated a job to be done?

- **Implementation risk.** Assuming a successful pilot, what do the implementation hurdles look like? How difficult will it be to turn the pilot's results into daily reality?
- **Access.** This means you have a solid, vetted lead who's willing to listen to a pitch and is empowered to act on it. That's the difference between true customer access and the mere convenience of "easy" candidates. The latter means that someone has a buddy or a connection who can perhaps open a door and arrange a meeting but lacks the overview of all the criteria we consider essential for selecting the strongest pilot candidates.
- **Transferability.** Achieving a great result is meaningless if you have no way to project the results to other customers in that segment or to a broader share of the market. The key is to find pilot customers who are representative of a segment. A small number of pilots with those companies will allow you to generalize your findings to a wider segment and accelerate your prospecting for future customers. They will also allow you to publish your first value story and establish your first credible references.

The process is detailed, but it's not rocket science. But it's much better than "I know someone who could do this with us"! Prepare a spreadsheet, select a preferred rating scale (e.g., 1–10 rating or 1–5 stars), and have multiple people with customer knowledge evaluate potential pilot partners. Depending on the size and concentration of your customer base, you should end up with a list of 10 to 15 customers who could be serious pilot candidates.

Striking the right balance in your pilot portfolio

But you can't simply truncate your evaluation list and assume that these 10 to 15 are your final, complete pool. There's another

(*main text continues on page 106*)

HPE Customer Pilots to Promote Value Stories

 HPE IoT solution to reduce unplanned downtime of an industrial manufacturing company

Context

HIROTEC selected HPE to pair their IoT solution with its manufacturing tools in order to enhance production capabilities and avoid unnecessary downtime. HIROTEC is an automotive parts manufacturer, building several millions of doors and exhaust systems per year.[1]

Current downtime (assumption)

- 700H of average downtime per year (average machine downtime per manufacturer in the automotive industry)

Automotive market challenges

- Decrease prices
- Maintain high quality

Benefits of the HPE IoT solution for HIROTEC

- Real-time visibility of operations
- Historical data analysis
- Failures prediction

Value driver and variables

Minimize unplanned downtime	▶ Enhance manufacturing capabilities with continuous operations
	▶ Reduce the time needed to manually inspect production systems
	▶ Ensure on-time deliveries for the customer

---

1   HPE: https://www.hpe.com/us/en/customer-case-studies/hirotec-iot.html

Savings

- 700H of average downtime per year[2]
- 20 percent of machine downtime reduction[3]
- Cost of a machine downtime per hour = $1.3M[4]

= $182M savings per year

(Public information extracted from the HPE website in May 2018)

---

2   eMaint: https://www.slideshare.net/emaintX3
     /costs-of-downtime-in-the-manufacturing-industry
3   McKinsey & Company: https://www.mckinsey.com
4   Survey by Nielsen Research, 2006.

(*continued from page 104*)
level of filtering you need to apply, which means weighting some of the criteria. In short, you need to strike a balance between a customer's digital maturity and your differentiation power. If you choose only the best of the best—the pioneering customers with high maturity and a record in digital growth initiatives—the odds are much higher that your competitors are either already working with them, or have left biases, reference points, and price anchors in their wake that you will need to overcome or dislodge. It may be harder for you to differentiate yourself or to build a sufficiently strong case for your differentiation.

Putting all your eggs in one basket is risky because of the intense competition for these high-value, commercially ready customers. Therefore, we recommend the approach shown in figure 5.2, which calls for a balance between medium- and high-maturity customers. You can often achieve this by focusing on a variety of applications.

The selection process will include a discovery stage. You'll have preliminary discussions, introduce yourself, and ask to do

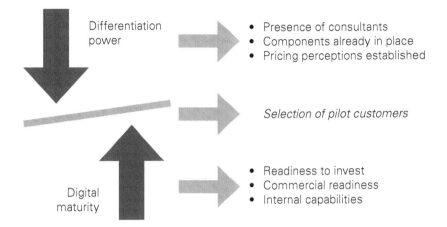

Figure 5.2. Balancing digital maturity and differentiation power for pilot selection.

some exploration with the customer. Fortunately, your efforts in reviewing your segmentation will find additional application in this step. You've already done homework on value-in-use analysis. It's now time to formalize and apply this information to the selection of pilot candidates.

Involving the customer: Preparation is everything!

You need to break the relevant customer processes into discrete parts and analyze them thoroughly. Think of this as a "day in the life of the customer" exercise. Who does what? What process steps are interconnected? What assets are used? Where are the pains and gains? You gain this understanding through observation (e.g., site visits, plant tours) and capture the insights in process maps, flowcharts, and timelines. You can then supplement this research with detailed interviews of key customer stakeholders involved at each level of the process.

This work will enable you to be thoroughly prepared to pitch, win, and conduct a pilot. You'll draw on your value-in-use analysis, support it with case studies, appeal to stakeholders' self-interests, and explain how your potential solution is superior to competitors'. This preparation is time-intensive and potentially tedious, but it's also indispensable forensic work. If you can't identify the job to be done, convince the customer that you thoroughly understand their key concerns, and have a concrete, viable offer to test, you haven't done enough work.

The customer will know whether you're prepared. Don't fool yourself. A little-discussed aspect is that pilots are a two-way street. The customer is piloting you as well. As we mentioned earlier, the digital offer you develop doesn't exist in isolation. Your potential pilot customer may have a dozen other companies knocking at their door with similar offerings aimed at the same job to be done that you've identified.

Pilot customers are taking a big chance when they work with you. You're asking to equip their plants, their core business, with sensors that can provide unprecedented detailed insights into what they do. You have to reassure the customer and sustain their confidence in their bet by demonstrating capabilities in risk management and the ability to validate every critical element of your value model. You have to help them define their own tradeoffs (upside vs. investment and risk) before they will grant you permission to access their assets and learn more about their business. A pilot can also be an emotionally charged subject; you'll be installing sensors, cables, connectors, and other devices that can expose vulnerabilities as well as strengths. This is why your pilot customer's perception of you as a trusted partner becomes a key factor in your successfully implementing a pilot project.

Conducting a pilot is ultimately a *mutual* decision, not just your decision. Each customer will have their own roadmap for the adoption of data-enabled services. They'll be defining their expectations, selecting their partners, testing solutions according to their own criteria, and deciding whom to work with over the medium and long term. The more you know about your customer's roadmap and how to qualify as a trusted partner, the better you can decide whether seeking to conduct a pilot with that client makes sense.

How long should a pilot last

Some customers equate digital with speed. This leads to the misconception that pilots will go incredibly quickly. This isn't necessarily true.

Think of how long it has taken for some of the best digital pioneers to scale their solutions to the billion-dollar sales level or greater. The process can take several years. The notion that you could go see a customer, introduce your digital platform or digital offer, and expect the customer to adopt it worldwide in a matter of three months is irrational and unrealistic.

In essence, it takes time. Most likely, in digital, every customer relationship will begin with either a pilot or proof of concept—which will involve at least six months of work, assuming the customer already has the needed digital maturity, infrastructure, skills, and data (revisit figure 2.8, where we present a typical customer selection process). But you want to do everything in your power to shorten the time. If you pick a small number of pilots with customers having low digital maturity, it could take years to extract results. But the better-prepared, experienced customers may accept pilots as short as 60 or 90 days if you've prepared thoroughly, as we described above. But remember that every customer will require a discovery process. They'll need reassurance and trust before they decide to commit and scale.

Who should lead your pilots

Imagine the worst-case scenario from a pilot. You conduct your work, and at the end of 60 days or six months the client says "thanks," offers you a small payment or reimbursement, and then decides to proceed on their own or to bring in a different partner with better implementation skills. How can you avoid such an outcome? It begins with appreciating the role of a pilot. You're not only testing your digital offer from a technical standpoint. Customer pilots are essential to preselling a larger scope of work. Your objective is to win the next step in the customer's process, not pave the way for a competitor.

The traditional salespeople in your core daily business cannot reasonably undertake deep, long, detailed customer pilots beyond their normal work. They lack the bandwidth and, in some cases, an appreciation for the speed and the acceleration that a project may require. So who will manage this portfolio of pilots? Who has the right technical, marketing, and management skills to run the project, work hand in hand with the customer to track the pilot, and define success and next steps?

That project leader needs to assemble a team to conduct the upfront forensics, prepare and win the pitches, conduct the pilots, and interpret and apply the results to something attractive and scalable. You can't afford a weak link in this chain. Leading a pilot requires an excellent project manager. An inability to stay on track, manage client expectations, or handle unexpected events in a customer pilot can kill even the most promising digital offer.

The process may seem overwhelming, but you have no choice. You have to pilot and gain external validation, because this isn't business as usual. Piloting requires a structured, intelligent, and proactive approach to data-enabled services that gives you an optimal set of customer pilots that you can complete in a timely fashion. In chapter 6, we discuss how to work with pilot customers effectively and efficiently.

Step 4: Put Your Offer in Co-incubation with Customers

For every one of our failures, we had spreadsheets that looked awesome.

—Scott Cook, cofounder and chairman at Intuit

NO COMPANY CAN SPEND millions to launch and scale a product or a data-enabled service that isn't supported by and validated with customer information and customer feedback. You've selected customers for pilots, but now you must execute. Involving customers in the *commercial prototyping* process is crucial, and speed is a key to success. You must get the most out of your time window, which could be as short as 30 to 90 days depending on your preparation and the customer's digital maturity, urgency, and commitment.

Following the pattern you've seen so far throughout the steps in the Data Monetization Roadmap, it's time for us to ask you some simple questions that have no simple answers, and then to give you a structured and proven way to answer them. Let's begin with the questions: What versions of your product or service do you bring to the pilot? What should your testing plan look like? What do you need to prototype beyond the actual product or service itself? How do you get the data, information, and insights that you need? And, finally, why is co-incubation a superior approach?

Framing your digital offer

Framing means putting a structured process around the market strategy and the technology that will allow you to move from ideation to prototyping, and then from your prelaunch to your launch phase. Most incubators will manage a technology framing process alongside a go-to-market framing process. They run in parallel and inform each other along the way. Fast and frequent prototyping is essential to framing your digital offer. Most companies will use some type of incubator, whether it's a factory, a lab, or another structure. Likewise, most will use one of several methodologies for framing digital offers. Here, we focus on the approach of developing an MVP. This lean approach has been adopted by many companies. It's fast, efficient, and effective and prevents your development team from overengineering your digital offer. MVP keeps the entire process focused squarely on what your customers really need.

Go-to-market framing requires a lot of work in parallel and an extensive toolkit. In previous chapters we explored framing aspects such as working through all aspects of the business model (the starting point for framing), customer segmentation, and the selection of your best pilot customers. Framing your digital MVP

(*main text continues on page 118*)

The Use of Canvases to Help Frame Digital Opportunities, *by Katie Richardson*

Early in the process of MVP development and framing, digital teams need to embrace the right methods, processes, and canvases. Digital leaders must choose canvases early during the formation of digital factories or digital incubators, and with care, using the following criteria:

1 Credibility of the creator(s) in the relevant subject matter: Alex Osterwalder, Eric Ries, and Stephan Liozu are thought leaders in their space
2 Degree of adoption in the digital ecosystem
3 Simplicity of canvas design and execution
4 Complementarity of the canvases (avoiding overlap or repetition)
5 Availability of digital content (paid or free) to raise skill levels

A business model canvas is defined in Wikipedia as "a strategic management and lean startup template for developing new or documenting existing business models. It is a visual chart with elements describing a firm's or product's value proposition, infrastructure, customers, and finances" (https://en.wikipedia.org/wiki/Business_Model_Canvas).[1]

Lean Canvas is "a 1-page business plan template created by Ash Maurya that helps you deconstruct your idea into its key assumptions. It is adapted from Alex Osterwalder's Business Model Canvas and replaces elaborate business plans with a single page business model" (https://leanstack .com/leancanvas). The Lean Startup canvas was created to give innovators a tool for applying the Lean Startup principles. The Lean Startup process, developed by Eric Ries, is a

---

1   All website excerpts as of May 5, 2018.

"scientific approach to creating and managing startups and get[ting] a desired product to customers' hands faster. The Lean Startup method teaches you how to drive a startup—how to steer, when to turn, and when to persevere—and grow a business with maximum acceleration. It is a principled approach to new product development" (http://theleanstartup.com/principles).

The Strategyzer canvas combines value proposition and business model canvases to better inform innovation and digital decisions. It is "a global standard used by millions of people in companies of all sizes. You can use the canvas to describe, design, challenge, and pivot your business model. It works in conjunction with the Value Proposition Canvas and other strategic management and execution tools and processes" (https://strategyzer.com/canvas/business-model-canvas).

The Pricing Model Innovation Canvas (PMIC) was developed by Stephan Liozu, the founder of Value Innoruption Advisors, to deep-dive into the revenue model block of Osterwalder's Business Model Canvas. The PMIC focuses on the 3 C's of pricing (cost, competition, and customer value) and a fourth C related to change management to support the design and execution of pricing models. The canvas describes the various methods, analyses, and outcomes of the 4 C's. It helps users select the proper pricing model(s) and the relevant pricing test plan and to make better-informed pricing decisions (http://www.valueinnoruption.com).

So there are plenty of well-established canvases available to use to frame digital MVPs. What are the benefits of using canvases as part of the digital framing?

1 They provide structure to digital teams who may be multifunctional and who might lack basic knowledge about go-to-market strategies.

2 They help you focus on the most critical elements of your MVP: Strategyzer focuses on critical partnerships and the types of customer relationships that are needed. Lean Canvas zeroes in on the "wow" differentiators and unfair advantages. The PMIC zooms in on the 4 C's of pricing.

3 They remind you of the important dimensions of the business model: framing an MVP requires discipline and comprehensive analysis. There should be no omissions or cutting of corners.

4 They focus on the design and execution of your MVP, essential in the digital space. Strategyzer and the PMIC focus equally on both.

5 They include a strong testing dimension: Strategyzer proposes testing of viability, feasibility, and desirability. The PMIC canvas discusses pricing research to test willingness to pay, pricing model options, and pricing levels.

6 They help bridge core business to the digital world: all canvases allow for more collaborative discussions, brainstorming blitzes, and strong alignment.

7 They open the door to different adjacent concepts and methods: for example, Strategyzer's culture and alignment maps can be added to the business model work to include the cultural dimension of change.

8 Canvases help frame the story: they don't replace a deep project plan or strategic business plan, but they help elevate the story to a higher level.

Remember that a canvas is just a canvas. Nothing will get done without research, curiosity, energy, coaching, and great facilitation. Having a good canvas coach is as important as having a canvas. Beware of the use of multiple and overlapping canvases in your factory or incubator. Pick one or two and rally the team around them while reinforcing consistency across teams. These should take the team from ideation to implementation of your MVP or proof of concept. Finally, make sure to provide enough training to digital teams so that they can appropriate and assimilate the tools for the framing process. You can't frame if you're still discovering the science behind this tool.

(*continued from page 114*)
requires segment-specific value propositions and a clear articulation of your differentiation: the "wow" factors that will define and establish your superiority in the customer's eyes. Then you'll need to write a value "equation" comprising critical value drivers and dollarize it using established tools such as EVE or TCP. Once you've developed a testing and validation plan, you'll need a plan for applying the results and insights: what are your internal business context, your assumptions, your risk assessment, and your overall vision for the solution? The final step—and one that many people incorrectly believe should be among the first—is reviewing your options for a pricing model, which could range from a traditional product-based model all the way to an outcome-based model.

We realize we're hitting you with a ton of bricks here, but this framing is essential. So we'd like to remind you of three caveats. First, there's no room for improvisation with respect to these tools and the steps in the process. You can't wing it, you can't spend your energy inventing shortcuts, you can't omit any steps, and you'll need to provide resources for the go-to-market framing process and not only for the technical one. Second, you can't do it alone. Partners are a must, and at this stage your most important partners are your customers. Third, you have to remember that you're in constant and intense competition for opportunities to be a provider of data-enabled services. Customers have no obligation to invest in your offer. They'll always look for next-best alternatives. You're on a constant mission to prove yourself and prove that your offering is superior.

Building a testing plan for your MVP

Let's assume that you have 90 days in a pilot to refine your MVP, including a value-driven go-to-market strategy and a digital pricing model. You need a plan that keeps you on track and rapidly generates the insights that you and your customer need for validation and improvement.

Our recommended plan in figure 6.1 is a mandate, not a menu. When you begin the process you'll have initial estimates and assumptions for each of these aspects, derived from your existing customer relationship and the homework you've done so far. Your digital development team, working closely with the pilot customer, will constantly refine each parameter and generate new ideas as you proceed until your MVP is the best it can be. This will require creativity and flexibility, but there's no room for improvisation in this comprehensive step-by-step plan. You can't neglect or fudge a step.

You'll see some very familiar aspects on the list, such as defining the critical jobs to be done and identifying customer pains

---

Testing plan for your MVP

- Customer's critical jobs to do
- Customer's biggest pains and gains
- "Wow"/true differentiators versus competition
- Performance and operational assumptions, value calculations, and savings potential
- Willingness to pay for options, modules, functionalities
- Pricing model preferences and willingness to accept
- Internal costing assumptions for solution, for integration in the customer process, and for service intensity
- Scaling plans and projections

Figure 6.1. What you must test.

and gains. Now the time has come to test real viable solutions for those problems, to verify and quantify your key points of difference, to understand how both you and your customer can operationalize your solution, and to choose the best pricing model. The question of which pricing model to use has no intrinsic answer. While the data may indicate, for example, that a subscription model is best, you'll run into difficulties if customers explicitly refuse to consider subscription models or will do so only at a price point that makes your data-enabled solution unattractive for you as a supplier. Or you may see an outcome-based model as ideal, but your pilot reveals that you can't yet measure performance precisely enough to create a viable pricing model.

You also need to test scaling plans, market assumptions, and projections in the pilot. This demands the deployment of a highly qualified team on your side and the participation of customers who are willing to share data and permit access to their assets. The customer becomes a partner and a stakeholder in your testing, which is how the idea of co-incubation works. Your customer also stands to learn a tremendous amount, so everybody wins.

The activities listed in figure 6.1 are generally expected if you've adopted a business modeling methodology. As you can imagine, they require budgets and skills. Digital natives tend to understand this and have progressive go-to-market approaches fueled by customer data. Industrial natives relying on digital factories or incubators will typically focus on the technology framing process and less on go-to-market framing. Most industrial companies staff their factories and incubators with scientists, IT professionals, developers, and operational people. Very few design their digital framing process with marketing and sales professionals and processes from the get-go. Then they play catch-up when they realize that most of the figure 6.1 deliverables were not properly prepared.

Fast prototyping: Make mistakes, recover quickly, and kill off bad ideas

The data-based offer itself is only one of many things you need to prototype and test. Every aspect shown in figure 6.2 requires a prototype or working assumption; all these aspects are tested and refined in parallel during the co-incubation period. You may begin with multiple versions of what your MVP could look like, depending on your segments, but we can assure you of two things regarding the outcome: each of your original MVP concepts will evolve (most of them beyond recognition), and not all of them will or should survive the co-incubation process.

Within a 30-day, 60-day, or 90-day timeline for rapid digital prototyping, it is naïve to think that this process will be smooth and linear. In fact, a process that proceeds in a smooth, linear fashion would make us highly suspicious of the assumptions, the data and analysis, and the quality of the output. Things will go

What needs to be prototyped

- The digital solution: product, software, architecture, etc.
- Product/solution strategic roadmap
- Good/better/best versioning strategy for the solution
- Integration plan for the digital solutions in the customer process
- User experience of the solution
- Dollarized value models for iterations of the solutions
- Pricing model options with internal and external impact
- Commercial process (tools, messages, incentives)
- Service support packages to respond to SLA requirements and expectations

Figure 6.2. You need a prototype or set of assumptions for much more than the solution itself.

wrong and will go off track. Things can get overlooked. The challenge is to make adjustments on the fly while maintaining the integrity of your pilot, bolstering customer trust and motivation, and staying intensely focused on solving the job to be done. This sounds a lot like the agile methodology, but we won't elaborate on that here. You'll have to make quick changes and quick pivots as the pilot uncovers new insights, validates some assumptions, and refutes others. That's why the pilot takes place in an incubator. You can make mistakes now rather than when you've transferred the offer back into the core business. The cliché about failing quickly may sound sexy, but it's misleading because it overstates what happens. We don't want you to fail. Mistakes are inevitable, especially when you and the customer are transparent and honest about what you observe. Success depends on how well and how quickly you adjust after those mistakes. That's the right culture and spirit of co-incubation.

Honesty and transparency place another requirement on you and the customer: you must kill bad ideas. Don't put them on life support, make excuses for them, or nurse them along. Only the most valuable ideas survive the process. You need to consider the framing process within a digital incubator as an innovation funnel with potentially only a few ideas turning into commercial launches. In other words, if 100 percent of the MVPs entering the funnel survive the framing process, the factory or incubators aren't doing their work. It's often much wiser to step back and withdraw a weak MVP, or even kill it, no matter how much you've invested in it. We're often shocked by how many teams surrender to the temptation to make up data, suppress bad results, or otherwise distort findings to ensure the survival of an idea and its team. You must challenge your team to come up with the right business model, to conduct the proper value assessment, and to test your assumptions rigorously and thoroughly. Applying a bandage and dragging the offer through the process only ensures that you'll transfer a flawed product to your core business. Nobody—except perhaps your competitors—wins when that happens. You must let go when faced with a shaky business model or a prototype that just doesn't sit right.

Getting the data, information, and insights you need

Customer involvement is one way to ensure that the best ideas emerge, take shape, and survive testing. Bringing customers on board early ensures that bad concepts die a rapid death. In our view, customer involvement and customer co-creation are most important. The answer to questions such as "How many people on the customer and market side should we talk to?" is almost always "As many as you can." Cast a wide net. Get out and talk to customers, different stakeholders in customers' organizations, customers' customers, industry leaders, and other relevant parties to test your hypotheses. Your team needs to remain focused on the pilot, regardless of their other responsibilities. This team must include subject-matter experts of all relevant functions, inside both your and the customer's organization, that touch on the critical issues related to developing, creating, and commercializing your digital offer. Carefully select your team lead, as (s)he will need to have excellent skills in aligning everyone around the common project goal—within a short time frame.

Another often overlooked source of information is independent research, especially on pricing. Compared to the turn of the 21st century—when McKinsey estimated that less than 10 percent of companies conducted it—pricing research is now much faster, orders of magnitude less expensive, and far more reliable. Figure 6.3 shows some options for testing your assumptions around a pricing model.

Pricing research can help to test your model options

- Willingness-to-pay research (quantitative or qualitative)
- Pricing model concept testing (expert interviews, focus groups)
- A/B testing of pricing structure for each version of the solution
- Discrete choice modeling (conjoint analysis for larger customer populations)
- Direct price testing methods (van Westendorp or Gabor–Granger methods)
- Pricing sensitivity research (quantitative or qualitative)

Feeds the economic benefit analysis for a digital service based on estimates of sales volumes, revenue, profits under various pricing and cost scenarios

---

Figure 6.3. You have many fast and reliable options for insightful pricing research.

Online surveys can generate hundreds of responses from customers in a few days for a few thousand dollars. Digital natives conduct such surveys every day; they see collecting data as integral to doing business, whereas digital immigrants often see data collection as something separate and additional. This perception needs to change. Industrial natives need to learn quickly how to adopt a quick and agile approach to customer research.

Why co-incubate with customers?

Co-incubation with customers is essential. The key part is the *co-*, which implies not only involvement and cooperation but true reciprocity. The two-way street should encourage an unobstructed and transparent two-way flow of data and information and a sharing of ideas, thoughts, and risk. The customer likely has many options for solving its problem, so a pilot isn't an open house for you to come in, browse around, and decide whether you'd like to stay. Both parties need to choose their partner judiciously. At the same time, the customer may lack the skills, resources, or risk appetite needed to resolve its job to be done on its own. To make such a partnership work, align your interests, have a governance structure and mechanisms in place, and help everyone learn from the co-incubation process.

When set up in the right way, co-incubation offers a company numerous advantages. The first is the creation of technical switching barriers, assuming you're the first company to pilot. The better your co-incubation project performs, the harder and costlier it will be for your customer to switch away not only from you but from the other partners you bring on board, say, for a cloud platform, security, or storage. This places special importance on the initial pilots, to make sure the partners within the network you've established can work together successfully and that you can begin thinking about how to scale it and how to sustain it.

Co-incubation allows you to validate your value-model assumptions. You're in learning mode. You may have estimated a certain parameter at 10 percent, based on your own internal work, but now you have a chance at the customer in a controlled environment, built on customer trust, to see whether that parameter is, say, at 8.5, 10, or 11 percent. This environment also allows you to test the resilience and flexibility of your prototypical offer. You'll inevitably identify gaps in the data pool and in the platform, and even confront production issues such as power outages or unplanned maintenance. How quickly can you recover and adjust after a mistake or glitch?

Being in a controlled customer environment also gives you a new baseline or "as is" situation for measuring both investment and performance. Can you perform the same job with fewer sensors or fewer data sources? Or do you need more? During the co-incubation process, you have an opportunity to establish the quality, accuracy, and veracity of critical data. The better and richer the data you collect, the better you can identify, understand, and explain variations or outliers later, should they occur. Customers, in turn, may also already collect reliable data that you haven't used yet in your own models, such as scrap rates, rejection rates, or performance quality. You can incorporate and test these as well.

In co-incubation you'll establish, track, and validate those metrics that matter most to your project. Together with customers, you'll select the most relevant KPIs or develop new ones. Measuring investment and performance with precision is indispensable, especially if you're considering an outcome-based performance component in your pricing model. Remember that your goal isn't to sell data or software. You want to sell insights, outcomes, or performance. Once you have a solid proof of concept and sound projections based on your customer pilots, you'll be in a strong position to design the most appropriate pricing model. If everything's under control and you have a very good predictive model, you may decide to give away both the software and the equipment and then charge the customer on a pay-as-you-go basis (pay-per-click, pay-per-mile, etc.) or based on an actual measurable outcome versus a baseline.

If you've inferred that measurability and trust are two underpinnings of a partnership with customers, you're right. Co-incubation is essential. It takes more time than you can afford to take but it's worth the investment. This may be one of the biggest frustrations we hear from digital teams in industrial companies. They spend lots of time and money co-incubating with customers, and the conversion to concrete scalable business opportunity is slow. The contradiction is real. On one side, the digital world is fast and dynamic. On the other side, we have to spend weeks and months testing, validating, and co-incubating.

In chapter 7 we explore measuring and quantifying the value of your solution (Step 5). Then, before we get to Step 6, we insert a separate chapter on building trust and confidence in the data and its value.

7

Step 5: Measure and Quantify the Value of Your Solution

The net effect of smart, connected products will be different in every industry, but across the board the nature of competition will change.
—Michael Porter, Harvard Business Review, *2015*

LET'S SAY FOR THE sake of argument that you can reduce a customer's operating costs by 15 percent while simplifying their user interface and customer interactions so dramatically that their churn loss decreases by 5 percentage points. We can appreciate your team's thrill and the sense of accomplishment that comes from learning that their new digital offer can provide significant cost savings and simultaneously offer the customer considerable revenue enhancements.

Now comes the cold water.

It's discouraging if a team then sees its offering rejected by the customer. This can happen if, say, a company outside your traditional set of competitors convinces the client that they can cut their costs by 23 percent and decrease their churn loss by 3 percentage points. The customer has decided that the significantly greater cost savings outweigh the upside potential from the slightly lower improvement in churn. As powerful as your solution is in absolute terms, it loses on a relative basis.

This is why, in addition to stressing customer intimacy (which would have told you that your customer values cost savings more than customer retention), we can't emphasize enough the critical role of competitive intelligence. Dollarizing your digital offer's differentiation—the focus of this chapter—is essential to success. But it's impossible to achieve this without knowing what your competitors are offering and expressing your differentiation value in dollar terms.

One of the most surprising findings of our research is the extent to which people underestimate or ignore competition because, for most of them, digital is still new. The reality is that many elements of the data value chain and its digital applications have been greatly commoditized over the last two or three years. There is fierce competition in the digital space, and it will only increase with the current rate of innovation and growing M&A activities. From working with executives, conducting expert interviews across industries, and reviewing well over 200 published reports, we learned that underestimating competition has different dimensions. Decision makers underestimate the sources, the intensity, and the relevance of competition. The tendency to underestimate competition when developing new offers isn't new. Over the years, we've noticed this common problem as one of the main hurdles to leading product and service innovation projects in a broad cross-section of industries. Recently, though, we've seen the need to incorporate competitors' moves into data monetization projects become even more pressing than before.

Competition redefined!

The growing digital tsunami has given customers many more transparent and available options. But we find that many companies, especially industrial natives, describe their data-enabled offers to customers in absolute terms, as if the competition didn't exist or the customer had not yet begun. This is not only surprising but also irrational. The constant message to your team should be that "we are not alone," because all your competitors are engaging in a digital transformation or at least claiming they are. Nonetheless, teams begin framing up their offer, analyzing their differentiation, and seeking their "wow" factors as if every customer in the world wasn't scrutinizing the market for alternative offers. We've seen suppliers act as if there were no real competition. The reality is sobering. While some manufacturers are still in the early stages of their digital growth journey, many large industrial groups have been developing digital offers and monetizing data through connected devices and predictive maintenance for years; some have accumulated experience and built their learning curve for over a decade now.

Who are you competing against when you propose a customer pilot and when you scale your solution? The answers may surprise you. Competition in data-enabled services is not only intense and multifaceted but also structurally different from competition in traditional industries. We illustrate those differences in figure 7.1.

The customer can choose to do nothing or seek alternatives to your digital offer in one of three areas, all of which may appear as a better next-best alternative. Let's briefly review these options:

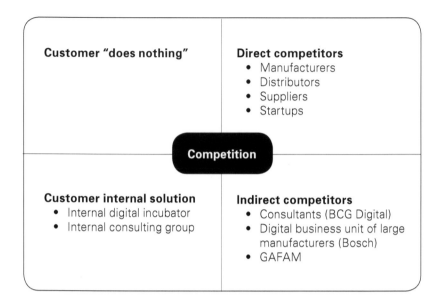

Figure 7.1. The extensive nature of digital competition.

- **Direct competitors.** Customers can choose a direct competitor offering software and data, and this type of competition is stratified. It could range from giants such as Siemens, Honeywell, Cisco, Intel, HPE, and Rockwell to very nimble startups, small manufacturers, industrial distributors, and systems integrators. All have digital initiatives. All are searching for ways to apply AI to resolve jobs to be done. All are pouring large sums of money into digital and making strategic acquisitions.
- **Indirect competitors.** This kind of competition is likewise stratified. They include the major global consulting firms (e.g., Deloitte and BCG) who sell billions of dollars' worth of digital transformations, platforms, solutions, and go-to-market services. Indirect competitors also include smaller, niche consulting companies focused on business transformation and

change management in the digital space. Indirect competitors also include the large digital business units of other manufacturers or conglomerates (e.g., GE Digital and Bosch Digital) that have begun to market their own expertise developed in-house. Finally, you must also carefully observe the moves of digital power players, such as Amazon or Google, as they continue to grow into the B2B space.

- **Customer internal solution.** Customers can often legitimately view a data-enabled service as a make-or-buy decision. This turns the customer into a competitor in its own right. Companies often decide that they don't want to turn to outside help to get the job done. In the digital space, we increasingly see B2B companies set up their own internal digital incubator, sometimes in conjunction with a consulting group. So you'll need to determine your differentiation from potential internal solutions as well. Industry experts concur that approximately 80 percent of companies today claim to have a digital transformation program underway. While this implies that 20 percent do not, these potential customers are not necessarily easy targets with limited knowledge of competition. Rest assured that even these customers seek knowledge about alternative suppliers and available options, assess their own internal capabilities, and are at least in the process of framing their decisions.

Complicating this further is the convergence already underway. We fully expect many current indirect competitors to become direct competitors within the next five to ten years. All they need is hardware, through either partnership, joint venture, or acquisition, and they will be on their way thanks to their existing speed and scale. Deloitte Digital is already offering turnkey IoT solutions within 90 days. How can Deloitte achieve results in such a short time? Together with deep customer focus, the company has a large and deep pool of talent, it has scale, and it forges critical partnerships and coalitions to secure needed strategic resources and capabilities.

This complexity and speed in digital competition means that when you craft your value proposition and develop your dollarized value models, you'll need up to four models, each with its own reference values. You may have to understand and dollarize your differentiation versus (1) direct competitors, (2) consulting companies, (3) a customer's internal benchmark, or (4) in some cases a generic "do nothing" option.

What is your basis for true differentiation?

We've both worked over many years with companies on understanding, quantifying, documenting, and communicating the superior value their offerings create for (and with) customers in business markets. Among the different value-based marketing and sales tools used, we refer here to the approaches and methods described in Stephan's book *Dollarizing Differentiation Value*. Among many commonly used tools, let's refer here to the well-known VRIO model, as it helps a firm to understand whether your digital offer can rely on one or more true point(s) of differentiation. The letters in the acronym VRIO, as we show in figure 7.2, stand for *Valuable, Rare, Imitate,* and *Organization.* The essence of this process, and the steps that follow, is identifying your differentiators and then focusing on those that are valuable to you and to your customers, that are rare and hard to imitate, and that you'll be good at executing.

Having a potential, meaningful competitive advantage boils down to how you answer the questions shown in figure 7.2. The most common and deceiving situation we see is the company that develops something with an indisputably high value in absolute

Data competitive advantage using the VRIO model

- Is it **V**aluable to customer in dollars and cents?
- Is it **R**are to find or access?
- Is it costly to **I**mitate?
- Is the firm **O**rganized to exploit it?

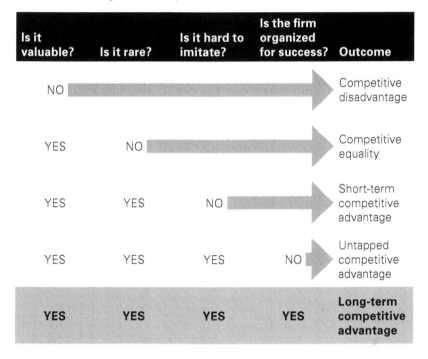

Is it valuable?	Is it rare?	Is it hard to imitate?	Is the firm organized for success?	Outcome
NO				Competitive disadvantage
YES	NO			Competitive equality
YES	YES	NO		Short-term competitive advantage
YES	YES	YES	NO	Untapped competitive advantage
YES	**YES**	**YES**	**YES**	**Long-term competitive advantage**

Figure 7.2. The VRIO model.

terms. But if that kind of solution is common, easy to imitate, and/ or hard for the organization to scale and sustain, that immense value is probably not the soundest basis for a competitive advantage. When you're scrutinizing competition to determine your relative position, the same questions and criteria apply. For all the talk and bluster you may read or hear about digital "solutions," many competitors will fall short because their organizations can't make the offering sustainable.

The VRIO model offers an understanding at the macro level, but the real understanding and action take place at the micro level. There are potentially hundreds of different aspects that a company could leverage to differentiate themselves and to create a competitive advantage. In each case, you'd need to find out whether direct or indirect competitors or the customer is better or worse than you. To provide some structure and to facilitate that thought process, we group the potential areas of advantage into five categories: data-based differentiators, analytics-based differentiators, business-model differentiators, value constellation differentiators, and pricing-based differentiators.

- **Data-based differentiators.** A first set of differentiators refers to the nature of data itself. These differentiators may be based on your ability to access, store, clean, and aggregate strategic data over time, including your data, the customer's, and data from external sources. Differentiation may flow from your ability to unite these different data sources under one roof. This explains why IBM acquired the Weather Company (former parent of The Weather Channel) and its extensive access to real-time weather data around the world. In a pilot, for example, the more data you have about an asset and its context, the better your scientific models can be. Then there is the question of integration: how well can you translate and incorporate data into one cohesive set?
- **Analytics-based differentiators.** These involve the applied research and science, the algorithms employed, and mathematics leveraged for analyzing data. You may have deeper research into AI, more advanced applied science, better algorithms, and more creative predictive models than other companies.
- **Business model differentiators.** All key building blocks of a digital business model can become the basis for

differentiation. Successful firms often focus on a more attractive value proposition than their competition, such as by promising outcome-based services that others cannot commit to. Companies also effectively differentiate themselves by focusing on specific customer groups that they serve better than others. Further, firms combine resources and activities in smarter ways than peers, thus decreasing costs and improving efficiency of operations.

The next two differentiators can be part of your business model differentiators. Because of their widespread ramifications, you can also consider them a source of differentiation in their own right.

- **Value constellation differentiators.** In this book, we dedicate an entire chapter to the strategic role of understanding your role in the business ecosystem and proactively managing your position in the data value constellation. As we've said many times, developing and managing the right digital platform depends on partnering with the right players. A potential customer will assess you by the "friends" you spend time with. Are you in the tight orbit of a Cisco, Microsoft, IBM, or Amazon, for example? Customers will also evaluate your access to other components and intelligent assets. Finally, they will judge you on your role in these partner networks. Are you a proven leader who can bring other, disparate suppliers together to solve a problem? This is another reason why being first to market is advantageous.
- **Pricing-based differentiators.** We dedicate an entire chapter in this book to value capture—that is, pricing. As we'll see, your pricing models may become a powerful source of differentiation. Choices in pricing, financing, and payment models, as well as service agreements, may set you apart from the competition. Does your company find new ways to share the

value pool with customers? Do you innovate in gain-sharing agreements with customers? What is a win-win for you, your customer, and potentially your partners?

We've listed only a few avenues for differentiation. The goal is to find the small set of unique points of difference for which your digital offer is truly and sustainably superior to your competitors' (direct, indirect, and internal) in the spirit of the VRIO model. Most digital factories and incubators lack the skills, time, and resources needed to conduct deep competitive analysis. It's frightening to see companies pour millions into technology without having a process and budget to conduct deep competitive benchmarking to discover which elements will thoroughly differentiate them from direct or indirect competitors. If you're about to launch an Industrial IoT solution, how do you know if what you're doing is better than what your direct competitors are doing? Recall the first paragraph of this chapter. You might be able to claim that your data-enabled solution will save customers 15 percent in operational efficiencies. But you have to know if your competitors are claiming that they can do a better job because of their unique design, relationships, and access to data. Maybe they've already committed to 18 percent in operational efficiency savings.

Choosing and using dollarization techniques

Dollarization is about translating your competitive advantage into financial benefits for customers. Approaches and techniques focused on value-based marketing and sales, especially in B2B market contexts, proliferated in the early 2000s.[10] During the

---

10   See, for example, James Anderson, Nirmala Kumar, and James Narus, *Value Merchants: Demonstrating and Documenting Superior Value in Business Markets* (Boston, MA: Harvard Business School Press, 2007).

same time, professional buyers increasingly emphasized TCO in sourcing decisions rather than focusing discussions solely around price. Translating the unique points of difference of your digital offerings into financial benefits for your customers is a key to commercializing your data resources and skills. Stephan's *Dollarizing Differentiation Value* likewise delves deeply into various dollarization techniques. Figure 7.3 enumerates some of the most common and powerful approaches, some of which we will illustrate (e.g., Economic Value Estimation, or EVE) in greater depth. We highly recommend that you do your own research on the one that seems most applicable to your situation.

TCO has a long history and is common in outsourcing decisions. TBO, discussed earlier in this book, is a newer approach that captures the revenue-generating benefits of a solution, not only the cost-savings aspect. The challenge that these models pose is to set a sufficiently long time horizon for your digital offering, because under some models you might lose money or barely break even as a supplier over the short term. Most of your upside is in the medium or long term.

Data Monetization Roadmap

TCO Total cost of ownership
TBO Total benefit of ownership
EVE® or CVM® models
LCC Life cycle costing analysis
LTV Customer lifetime value analysis
ROI Customer ROI calculation

EVE is a registered trademark of Monitor Company Group Limited Partnership. CVM is a registered trademark of Value Innoruption Advisors LLC.

Figure 7.3. Dollarization techniques.

The objective of EVE is to begin with a reference value and then add and subtract the values of your significant differentiators until you arrive at the net differentiation value that your solution generates. We also refer to this as the value pool. This model stands out because it includes the negative aspects as well. Part of being honest and transparent with customers is acknowledging where your solution may have drawbacks or deficits relative to alternatives, even though your overall solution is superior on an aggregated basis. This laddering process is shown in figure 7.4.

EVE has an elegant simplicity, but it also has an additional advantage. As a straightforward and easy-to-understand software tool, it allows you to ensure a common system when you're testing a large number of MVPs. When you have 75 or 100 or even more MVPs in testing, you can't afford to let each team adopt its own model, or its own way of applying a common model. This

(main text continues on page 144)

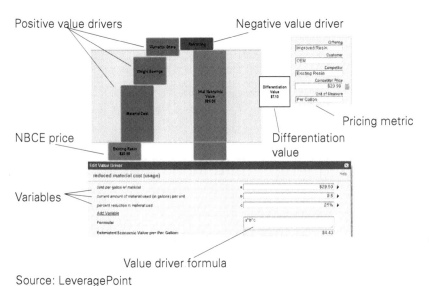

Source: LeveragePoint

Figure 7.4. An EVE example.

Dollarizing CloudLine, a Cloud Infrastructure Platform, *by LeveragePoint Innovations*

The value of cloud services is central to any enterprise embarking on the digital transformation journey. CloudLine is a representative (but fictional) infrastructure platform that provides significant benefits to organizations migrating from a predominantly on-premise approach to hosting and maintaining their business applications in the cloud. This value proposition was created to highlight the benefits of that transformation and to demonstrate the net value of implementing a new approach.

The CloudLine team identified four major problems for strategic IT managers that their solution addresses: (1) IT costs, (2) the time and delays involved in deploying new digital applications, (3) downtime, and (4) worker productivity. They then set out to quantify the value of four economically distinct value drivers arising from these problems based on interviews and surveys of seven customers who had implemented their solution.

For each of these four value drivers, the team came up with a simple approach to calculating value based on

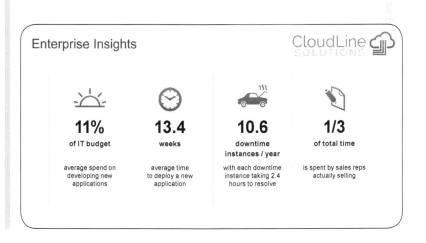

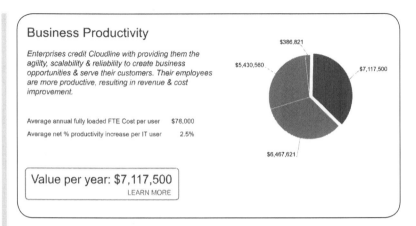

Business Productivity

Enterprises credit Cloudline with providing them the agility, scalability & reliability to create business opportunities & serve their customers. Their employees are more productive, resulting in revenue & cost improvement.

Average annual fully loaded FTE Cost per user $78,000

Average net % productivity increase per IT user   2.5%

$386,821
$5,430,560
$7,117,500
$6,467,621

Value per year: $7,117,500
LEARN MORE

benchmark data and a few key operating parameters that any CIO should be able to provide their sales representatives: number of users, number of business applications, number of virtual servers, and total IT staff. The first value driver was based on business productivity improvements. This value was estimated based on the number of IT users, average fully loaded FTE costs, and the net productivity increases per user observed by their survey participants who had implemented CloudLine.

They quantified infrastructure costs based on server and rack hardware costs, annual maintenance costs, annual software license costs, and annual facilities operating costs, again based on their interviews. Their second value driver, infrastructure cost reduction, was estimated as the impact of migrating to the cloud on these infrastructure costs over a three-year horizon based on the experience of their interviewees.

Their third value driver was based on improvements in IT staff productivity. In this case they considered separately the IT staff costs involved in maintaining on-premise infrastructure and the IT staff costs incurred in deploying new applications, because the costs per FTE were different and because their demonstrated impact on productivity was different. The value of staff productivity improvements for maintenance personnel and deployment personnel was based on the experience they typically saw from their survey participants.

Their fourth value driver was risk mitigation, where they focused primarily on user downtime. Based on the average experience of their interviewees, they estimated downtime per user per year prior to CloudLine deployment and downtime experience after deploying CloudLine, applying these average reductions across the user base at the fully loaded cost of an FTE.

The total resulting value that CloudLine creates can be seen in financial form quantitatively and graphically, in a value waterfall. This demonstrates a strong bottom-line impact, net of CloudLine's price, on an annual basis and over a multiyear horizon. This value proposition supports the CloudLine team as they establish and validate a business case for customers to buy their solution. CloudLine's sales representatives use the resulting value proposition as a case study for customer conversations early in the sales process. They use the value proposition to support a shared business case to buy Cloud-Line as their customer sponsors evaluate solutions and move through their internal approval and procurement process.

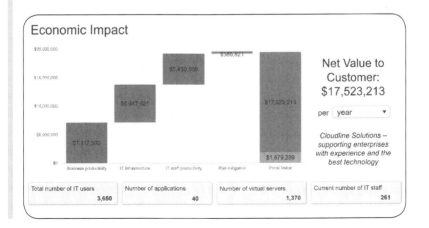

(continued from page 140)
will lead to confusion and make decisions across offers difficult, if not impossible, because of the diminished comparability when it's time to allocate resources and select which MVP will go to the next step. Even if you develop your own model, putting it on an automated platform is essential. Our experience with the framing process suggests that, just as you'd choose a specific business model framework for your framing, you should also select one or two dollarization techniques to include in the framing process. By doing so, you'll also industrialize your value modeling process and make it easy for MVP teams to learn one or two techniques, maximum. *(main text continues on page 148)*

Creating Value Models to Convey Value Stories, by *Value Innoruption Advisors*

Use case 1 Value proposition of an IoT solution for the mining sector[1]

Context

Given low current market prices and increased complexity of operations, mining companies need to maximize their production, optimize their process, and increase safety for their operators. Connected machines can help miners save several $M per year. According to PwC, big data is one of the top 5 priorities for miners in the years to come.

Solution: GE Predix, IoT solution

Benefits

- Increase production
- Reduce energy consumption

---

1   GE: https://www.ge.com/digital/sites/default/files/What-is-a
     -digital-industrial-company-infographic.pdf

- Reduce reagent consumption
- Reduce yield loss
- Increase recovery

Value drivers

- Asset utilization
- Operations optimization
- Business-wide optimization

Value model (per mining company, per year)

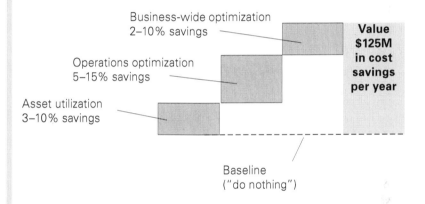

Business-wide optimization
2–10% savings

Operations optimization
5–15% savings

Asset utilization
3–10% savings

**Value
$125M
in cost
savings
per year**

Baseline
("do nothing")

Use case 2 Value proposition of an IoT solution for a medium-sized refinery in the US[2]

Context

Honeywell connects processes, assets, and workers to give customers a fully connected plant. According to Honeywell, its IoT solution can deliver (for a medium-sized refinery company) a minimum of $26M savings per year.

---

2   Honeywell: https://www.honeywellprocess.com/library/news
      -and-events/presentations/2017-HUG-Explore-How-an-IIoT
      -Ecosystem.pdf

Solution: HPS IoT solution

Benefits

. . . of Connected Process
- Deep domain expertise
- Optimization and analytics via the digital twin

. . . of Connected Assets
- Broad ecosystem of expertise and capabilities
- Predictive asset performance, increase uptime, decrease downtime

. . . of Connected Workers
- Enhanced decisions via data analytics
- Worker safety and compliance

. . . of Connected Plants
- Unmatched industry offering
- Integrated solutions that span the entire enterprise

Value drivers

- Maximize plant throughput
- Improve plant availability
- Protect knowledge

Value model (for a medium-sized refinery in the US, per year)

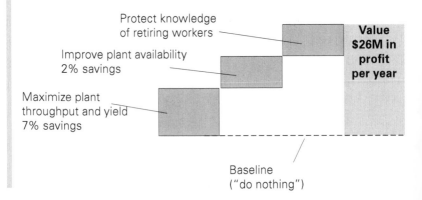

Protect knowledge of retiring workers

Improve plant availability 2% savings

Maximize plant throughput and yield 7% savings

Value $26M in profit per year

Baseline ("do nothing")

Use case 3 Average value proposition of an IoT solution[3]

Context

Instead of using isolated sensors for remote monitoring of assets, Siemens's IoT strategy focuses on transforming the entire manufacturing value chain, driving savings in unlimited fields.

Solution: Siemens MindSphere

Value drivers

- Operation optimization
- Predictive maintenance
- Inventory optimization
- Worker health and safety

Value model (for a classic IoT solution, based on McKinsey insights)

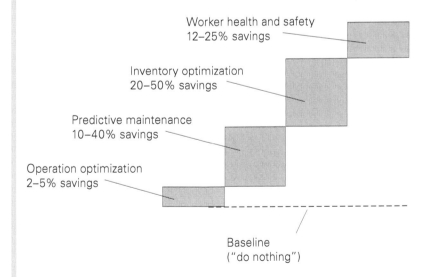

Worker health and safety
12–25% savings

Inventory optimization
20–50% savings

Predictive maintenance
10–40% savings

Operation optimization
2–5% savings

Baseline
("do nothing")

---

3   Siemens: http://www.siemens.com

(*continued from page 144*)

Difficulties in dollarizing data-driven offers

As straightforward as some methods (e.g., TCO, TBO) or tools (e.g., EVE) may be, we don't want to imply that dollarization itself is straightforward. There are many unknown variables in the digital world, and we haven't come across resounding success stories. So, you might encounter many difficulties in this process:

- **Lack of access to customer application data.** Regardless of the level of your customer intimacy, some of your digital opportunities might require access to operational data from different stakeholders. If you can't identify or access a data source, it will be hard to derive KPIs and determine their value.
- **Lack of deep knowledge of competitors' digital offerings.** You may know your competitors' traditional products and services in detail, but how well do you know what they're "cooking" in their digital incubators? Beyond what you can find publicly, even the richest and most reliable competitive intelligence may fail to give you a complete picture.
- **Your technical solution isn't fully conceptualized yet.** Digital pipeline development means that MVPs are in constant iteration. The more disruptive they are, the harder it can be to compare performance with that of competitors' offers, and the harder it may be to see precisely how your concept drives value in day-to-day reality.
- **Lack of test methods to evaluate performance in application.** Some of the features and benefits of your digital opportunities and data might be so new that you can't find an appropriate model for testing. Your team may need to develop new methods and metrics for measuring and extracting value.
- **MVPs might be complex systems or solutions.** Innovative digital offers frequently integrate multiple components

from complex hardware and software elements to value-added services. Measuring the combined value of such complex integrated offers can be a challenge.

We highlight these difficulties to preface the next step: value modeling. This is where words and concepts and high-level estimates are transformed into numbers, such as ratios, fractions, or percentage differences. These are then expressed in terms of hard money. This is another topic covered in greater detail in *Dollarizing Differentiation Value,* so we summarize it in the next section.

Value modeling: Expressing relative value in money terms

This next step helps you calculate dollarized value in an extensive, elaborate way. The sequence is to walk your customers through the differentiators and the benefits, highlight the most critical and compelling benefits, turn them into ratios, and then express them in monetary terms. The process is inherently mathematical, but it's an art as well as a science. Figure 7.5 lists the steps.

Approach to customer value modeling

1 **Translate** differentiators into customer benefits (using customer vocabulary, thinking process, mental frames)
2 **Prioritize** customer benefits based on segment (most compelling hook and last impression)
3 Turn these benefits into compelling **facts** and ratios (% faster, increase of 2 points of yield, 1/3 more durability)
4 **Dollarize** these benefits into $, £, ¥ or euros (dramatic numbers, round numbers, compelling savings/gains)
5 Create your **value story** or value script

Figure 7.5. The sequence of steps in customer value modeling.

The science lies in the mathematics and the mechanism for processing and calculating the value, formulas, and data. The art lies in how you prioritize your customer benefits, plus the nature of the numbers and the stories you tell around them. You can express your benefit as a ratio or a fraction, or devise a number that optimally blends art and science in a way that convinces the customer. This is not necessarily a skill that a team will possess, so accomplishing this requires training and practice.

The process of dollarizing an MVP is difficult and requires effort and creative thinking. Another challenge is finding relevant reference points. If what you're doing is relatively new, what are the credible and established references against which to measure yourself? If you don't have a customer-specific reference available, fortunately you can turn to other sources for credible guidance:

- **Published digital case studies and industry reports.** They often provide credible references on which to base your calculations. In figure 7.6 we provide some hard numbers that we've distilled from our review of over 200 reports. Because of previous independent validation or usage, these numbers are often better than theoretical calculations, no matter how logical or well derived the latter may be. We also suggest that you remain on the lookout for additional nuggets such as these.
- **Theoretical calculations based on technical assumptions.** Your technical and R&D teams might have test data or theoretical models, based on traditional customer operations. In the absence of independent external sources, these numbers can still provide a solid reference basis.
- **Academic research in the particular end-use application.** To generate some empirical data, you can collaborate with a university research center and sponsor an academic study generating data and providing results produced by a

Year	Method	Level (%)	Source
2018	Reduced customer churn in telecom operations through data analytics	15	McKinsey: Maximizing Value from Advanced Analytics in Telco Service Operations
2018	Reduction in asset maintenance costs	25	ServiceMax: 12 Facts You Need to Know About IoT
	Reduction in downtime	35	
2018	Increased OEE (availability, performance, quality)	5–15	Deloitte: Predictive Maintenance and Asset Monitoring
	Reduced unplanned downtime	15–30	
	Increased throughput and on-time delivery	10–20	
	Reduced maintenance costs	20–30	
	Improved quality	10–35	
2018	Reduced reactive maintenance	10–40	Deloitte: Asset Performance Management
	Improved employee productivity	5–5	
	Reduced environmental health and safety incidents	3–4	
	Reduced IT costs	5–25	
	Increased asset availability	2–6	
2018	Reduced finished goods and component inventory	3–5	Deloitte: Asset Tracking
	Increased operations labor efficiency	4–7	
	Increased quality labor efficiency	4–7	
2017	Reduction in time to market	≤50	Siemens Digital Manufacturing: The Race to a Digital Future
	Reduction in engineering costs	40–50	Raj Batra, President, Digital Factory Division, Siemens USA
2017	Downtime reduction for operators using predictive, data-driven approaches	36	Momenta Partners Ag: Realizing the the Opportunity in Predictive Maintenance Analytics
2017	Increase in truck production by collecting and analyzing machine data	25	Roland Berger: Mastering the Industrial Internet of Things

Figure 7.6. Sources of benchmarks for a "versus do nothing" analysis.

third party. You can also collaborate with a PhD student who can set up experimental research and run trials with customers. Many companies choose this alternative for the areas of smart seeds and the agricultural IoT. Whether you sponsor them or not, published academic papers can be used as credible sources of data.

- **Comparisons from other similar contexts.** In some cases, the "wow" differentiation of your MVP may be entirely new in one context but similar to solutions that companies have provided in other areas. You might have to scan outside your narrow industry for such analogs or to draw correlations. Data from a connected-car environment, for example, may apply to solutions in a rail transportation environment. You may sometimes need to make a leap of faith, but there is still an underlying logic.
- **Make assumptions to be tested with customers.** When nothing else works, you must work collaboratively with very friendly customers who have the same dilemma and who would welcome a joint solution. Develop your assumptions but involve customers in checking their robustness. The two main downsides are that this process can take time and may be subject to strict confidentiality, which limits its applicability to other customers.

What are the potential financial benefits from investing in digital initiatives? When culling data from a broad cross-section of consulting reports, industry analyses, and white papers, we found general agreement among diverse experts that the upsides in comparison to "doing nothing" are substantial (figure 7.6).

If you're working on an MVP and you don't know the reference value basis or a potential value difference to target and beat, you can use these credible sources as a first hook to convince your customers that the differentiation value in your solution can be substantial.

Let's say that a digitally savvy customer who knows you from your traditional business is leaning toward conducting a pilot with you but also has a do-nothing option on the table. The numbers in figure 7.6 should be significant enough to convince them to pursue collaboration. Then your task is to convince the customer to work with you and not with a direct or indirect competitor. Keep in mind that everything—from the savings generated by an offer to the advantage of faster time to market—can be dollarized. That is the nitty-gritty of dollarization.

The must-do tasks for dollarization

Throughout this chapter we've referred to data points, assumptions, and the need to test and validate. This puts the onus on you to be as meticulous as possible in recording and documenting every step of the process. This begins a mix of the "art" and "science" of dollarization, as you put your solution or your MVP into context for the customer. Defining the context is analogous to mapping your value constellation. You need to have an overview of all touchpoints, all relevant sources and types of data, and all interdependencies. The best way to do this is to bring a team together across different disciplines and functions, from AI to data analysis to marketing research, sales, and customer support. Include competitive intelligence experts in your team. We cannot understate that last point. Someone needs to study all relevant competitors (direct, indirect, and internal; current and future) in the digital space to know exactly what they're promising or what they're reasonably capable of. You must stay focused on the simplest question that matters: what makes you better than someone else at solving the job to be done? If your best answer is the size of your team or the number of your pilots, you're on the wrong path. If your answer is currently only in absolute terms, you need to put it in a relative context for it to be meaningful. Differentiation is always relative.

During the dollarization process you need to list *all* your assumptions, document *all* your calculations, and document *all* your data sources. Documentation and validation are key as you iterate until you've defined your value pool, the aggregate value of your dollarized differentiation. Once you have an initial number that you can support and document with confidence, that number goes to a process owner, who continues iterating and validating. The process owner is also responsible for ensuring that you always have a single current version of your model to avoid confusion or multiple parallel tracks.

By now, your journey on the Data Monetization Roadmap has shown you how dramatically different a data-enabled world is from your traditional business. From how you define value to how you embrace customers to how you create and quantify value, you need a systematic approach. You require many team interactions as well as testing and validation. But data monetization would not be complete without capturing a fair share of value created for customers. The step of getting paid for value created concludes the customer value cycle of understanding, creating, documenting, delivering, communicating, and capturing value. The final steps of the roadmap focus on pricing, implementation, and scaling. But before we get there, we need to focus on trust as the fundamental enabler of this process.

8

Build Confidence and Trust in the Data and Its Value

Industrial giants have well-established brands, built strong customer relationships, and signed long-term service contracts. They've won the customer's trust, which is why customers are willing to share data. Digital natives can work with industrial customers, but they have to first earn their trust; they must build capabilities to understand customer operations; they must match the industrials' cumulative learning from customer interactions; they must learn to ask for the right data; and they have to hire experts in several verticals that can turn data into insights.

—*Vijay Govindarajan,*
Harvard Business Review, *February 3, 2018*

THE FURTHER YOU ADVANCE along the Data Monetization Roadmap, the deeper your interactions with customers become and the more you'll have to focus on fostering customer trust. Your ability to build the customer's trust in your work, your data, and your digital approach can serve as a powerful and decisive differentiator. Trust may be the ultimate differentiator and the ultimate prerequisite for everything we discuss here. No company will let you conduct pilots, grant access to its data, and perform validation work in the absence of trust.

Deep knowledge and a good relationship are neither synonymous with trust nor a guarantee that you'll gain it. What do we mean by customer trust? It derives from all the elements we show in figure 8.1. The top three buckets in figure 8.1 must all be clarified at the outset of a customer interaction. You must also try to convince the customer that the top three buckets represent an ethical obligation for you and your company, not merely one governed by the letter of clauses in a contract.

Data quality. Projecting an understanding of data quality— what's needed, in what state, in what form, and so forth—is an important step in establishing confidence that the customer is providing data to a knowledgeable and trustworthy partner (namely, you). A factor key to successfully monetizing data is a supplier's ability to access and secure "clean" data. When working with B2B companies on growing their service portfolios beyond traditional B2B services into new data-driven offerings, one of the main hurdles we typically face is lack of clean data, or data that can be commercially leveraged. For example, one manufacturer collected historic equipment performance data, but selected data were missing. In other instances, data sources were incompatible. As a consequence, the supplier found it impossible to develop a data-enabled service in the short run. Think back to our example of Vixxo in chapter 3. The company gained a unique competitive

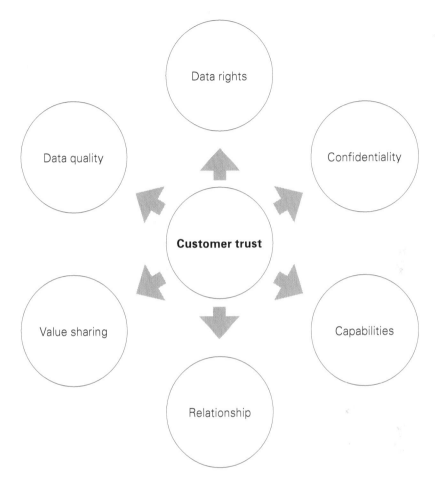

Figure 8.1. The elements of customer trust.

advantage, and a central position in the value constellation, because of its thoughtful anticipation and systematic collection of clean data in facility management, an industry where other players had not realized, early enough, that data was the foundation of next-generation competitive advantage.

Data rights. Trust builds on much more than that specialized knowledge. Another decisive factor you must address proactively is data protection and data management. You can't wait until you're deep in the process or address problems reactively after they occur. Customers are on edge, and rightfully so, in the wake of headlines about data breaches and misappropriation. Losses in market capitalization show that the issue extends beyond reputational damage with one customer. Any breach, misappropriation, or act that undermines customer trust can also undermine the entire market's trust in your business. What do you do with the data? How will you protect your customers' interests when they give you access to their data and share detailed information about their internal processes? B2B companies have to do their homework and formally address data rights at the beginning of the customer discussions. There needs to be strong alignment between all parties to avoid issues during the multiple stages of the relationship.

Confidentiality. This leads us to confidentiality, which you'll codify in contracts but must also proactively preserve. One potential leaky area is the underlying perception that data may be used by the supplier on an anonymized basis to develop reference cases for conducting benchmarking studies. Many of the firms we work with today on data-driven services to help customers improve their productivity include a benchmarking component. Decision makers are keen to compare their company's performance with that of industry peers: How does workflow in our hospital compare with that of other hospitals of similar size and operations? How does our offset printing machine compare with next-best alternatives? How about energy efficiency in our hotel versus similar hotels statewide? The ability to benchmark against industry standards is highly valued by many customers. Yet, if you're to be able to pool data, and perform benchmarking analyses, customers must trust you. Here, too, it's better to draw the lines around such usage in advance.

Capabilities. The customer must also develop a level of trust in your capabilities. The question "What will you do with the data?" is about not only purpose and intent but also process and capabilities. You must convince customers that you genuinely have the right business model, partners, and analytical capabilities. This is about your team too, not just your technology. In the course of your early explorations with customers, key customer contacts need to see and experience firsthand that the quality of your algorithms, your data integration software, and so forth are so robust that at minimum you have no shortcomings relative to other potential suppliers. Your incubators, your AI packages, and your other tools must be straightforward, compelling, and crystallized into well-crafted documents so that you manage the customer's perception and give them no cause for concern. They should have no sense that you are improvising, guessing, or using the customer as a guinea pig.

As far as the team is concerned, you need to meet the customer at eye level. When you have an opportunity to demonstrate your capabilities and shape the customer's perception, which experts are part of the team from your side? Do you include someone from business development as well as a marketing manager from the core business? Do you send your digital champion and other key subject-matter experts (e.g., AI)? Your choice of team members for these interactions should reflect your understanding of the customer's business model and organization, your assessment of the buying center, and your customer segmentation (see chapter 4). The savvier and more advanced the customer is, the higher-caliber experts you need to bring to the team, in terms of both subject-matter expertise and numbers. While we can't give you a firm rule of thumb, we can say from experience that the ratio of team members (customer's to yours) and the relative level of expertise (customer's to yours) make a powerful impression, because they signal how seriously you're taking the customer's job to be done and how qualified you are to solve it.

That raises a critical question about the required balance of skills. Does experience in the customer process and application trump experience in the data and digital space? It will depend on your customer sophistication, but generally speaking, it will be easier to get the attention of technical and manufacturing engineers in plants and around assets if you can speak their language and if you've been working in the field for 20 years. Deep customer application experience is potentially one of the key differentiators of industrial natives, as mentioned in chapter 7. This is why customer and field application engineers will be essential to your digital success, as they help you create customer trust.

Relationship. The discussion of team composition leads us to the relationship, another key constituent of customer trust in the digital space. This is a question of personal conduct and interaction, not merely of process management or of maintaining eye level with the customer. From the process side, you need to decide how many touchpoints you'll have with the customer throughout the process. Very often we see the customer business development manager making contact with multiple people at one big potential customer. That may make sense from the standpoint of efficiency, but it falls well short in terms of building trust and managing perceptions. Your relationship management system needs to account for numbers and eye level. When should your CEO have contact with the customer's CEO? When do your data scientists speak to theirs? This requires careful advance planning as well as tracking and monitoring. Finally, personal conduct is also a component of fostering trust. You have to ensure that any team you send—especially from the technical, data science, or research side—has not only the technical competence but also the social and emotional intelligence to engage the customer and represent your company, your data-enabled offering, and the client's interest in a positive and reinforcing way.

Value sharing. The final component of customer trust is the perception of value sharing. We argue that this begins with a humble approach to selling yourself. You must walk a very fine line. On one hand, you want to convincingly convey that you thoroughly understand your customer's business and key performance metrics. On the other hand, you don't want to come across as wanting to lecture your customer on how they could run their business so much better with your data-based offer and support. Several companies that we worked with faced outright rejection, from customers' middle management or frontline managers: "Are you telling me how to run my business?" is a question you don't want to hear. Another is "If I could really save 45 percent in operational savings so easily, I would have done it already." So, be mindful about how you deliver value propositions and savings to people who've been in the business for decades. Building customer trust means avoiding being cocky or arrogant—no matter how true your claims may be—because this could also cause the customer to think that you intend to lock-in customers, possibly overcharge them for your "premium" offer, or—in the worst case—capture the lion's share of joint value created. That impression, whether stated or not, plants doubt in the customer's mind and encourages them to keep their eyes open for alternative suppliers and different offers. This is precisely what you want to avoid!

You need to align interests from the beginning. Clearly convey early on that this partnering relationship has a strong win-win potential, that you will discover and validate the data-driven offer in close collaboration with the customer, and that benefits and expenses will be shared fairly. You can't press the client to do extra work without compensation. You can't insist that the customer provide you success stories or testimonials without something in return.

Those are the six key drivers of customer trust. But how do you pursue them in practical terms? From our extensive research and experience, we've distilled a set of best practices for building customer trust in the digital world.

- **Reflect your level of preparedness in your value proposition.** You'll project competence and build customer trust when your preparation shows underlying professionalism. This means that your value proposition must be clearly articulated in documents, with crisp names and straightforward language. Your presentation should anticipate questions and concerns and counter them confidently. Each step you take and each statement you make must support the impression that you know what you're talking about and can execute it for that customer.
- **Present success stories.** This doesn't mean bragging about how you saved some Fortune 500 company 25 percent of its costs in one area. A success story is literally that: a *story* about *success*. If you tested your concepts and prototypes internally on your own assets first, how did that process go? What did you learn, especially the hard way? Your stories must be real, humble, and credible. Customers love to hear about how your struggles can make them more successful faster, because you learned something they can profit from.
- **Provide credible and relevant customer value analysis.** Do your homework and convey to the customer that you know their value constellation and the broader equation your work will influence. Combining your previous work and success stories, you can craft a powerful message: you know the

ins and outs, but you also respect that every customer is different. That means that you and the customer will learn together, and that you can help them avoid the pitfalls and the traps you've overcome in the past.

- **Proactively address data issues.** Recognize, define, and proactively address all the relevant data issues, including cybersecurity. It all boils down to how you answer that deceptively simple yet multifaceted question: what will you do with my data?

- **Provide an end-to-end roadmap for collaboration.** The customer needs to understand, step by step, what it means to work with you. You and the customer will travel together on the journey of conceptualizing, validating, testing, and scaling your offer. Your customer value analysis and your experience should enable you to develop an effective and efficient blueprint for the collaboration. The more those plans help reduce the stress on the customer side, the better your relationship will be.

- **Show your strengths.** Bring your experts and partners to the table. This shows not only that you have deep alliances behind your digital offer but also that you have access to outside data. This brings strength and credibility to your story. It's the only place where name-dropping—assuming you have the context honestly defined—is recommended and works to your advantage in enhancing customer trust.

- **Adopt a position of fairness with respect to value and cost sharing.** We elaborated on this point in the previous section and refer to it here for completeness' sake.

A common thread in all these points is your ability to err on the side of humility and to avoid creating any impression of arrogance or cockiness. That's easy for us to say. But how do you help a team walk that line so well that it becomes second nature? A key part of that approach is to keep everything you propose, do, and demonstrate focused on the success of the customer.

Place your primary focus on customer success

As a supplier of digital offers, of course you want to succeed. Success affects not only your finances and your market valuation but also your reputation as a sought-after partner and a great place to work. Ultimately, however, you won't succeed on any of these dimensions if the customer is not successful first. This is why one of the booming professions in the software industry is called *customer success.* This function enables and energizes customer development and deployment while focusing on promised value. Figure 8.2 summarizes key elements that allow you to stay focused on putting customer success first in your data monetization initiative. Some of these steps are analogous to what you'd do in a traditional business environment.

Quick wins. As in every strategic initiative, quick wins still matter in a digital world as a means to establish trust and

---

The priority is to focus on customer success

- Focus on **quick wins** for early confidence in the project
- **Think small** in your initial steps, but scale in the vision
- Focus more on value **extraction** and value **validation** instead of pricing in the first 90 days
- Give **credit** for value capture to the customer team
- Be ready to absorb unexpected small expenses in order to move the project forward and show **goodwill**
- Your legal team should not be the **lead** of the process once the project is launched

Figure 8.2. How to stay focused on customer success.

confidence. These not only represent validation and proof of concept but also give the customer a basis for calculating and calibrating their own ROI from this joint effort. The challenge with quick wins is to take small initial steps while also scaling your vision. The pursuit of quick wins from small steps risks becoming shortsighted without the articulation of the longer-term vision— the completion of the job to be done—still serving as a guide.

Think small. Building on the idea of quick wins, a focus on customer success also means that you shouldn't hesitate to think small in your initial steps and scale up to the vision later on. In the early stages, it's important to scope your project so that both you and your customer feel confident that agreed-upon goals can be reached. Once you've reached your intermediary milestones on a smaller scale, you need to scale up. Will your offer ramp up to a larger scale? Will you be able to industrialize your data-driven offer to achieve the broader, more ambitious goals you've set with your customer?

Value extraction and validation. We've said many times that it's a mistake to focus on pricing very early in the data monetization process. This becomes explicitly clear in this context. In the first few months of your interaction, you need to focus on value extraction and validation rather than on the mechanics of pricing. Your objective should be to calculate and validate the size of the value pool and maintain the customer's confidence that that value will ultimately be shared fairly. Save the pricing discussion and the sharing mechanism for later. If the customer asks about pricing or gets curious, help them understand that you can't answer pricing questions without first answering value questions definitively. This is why choosing the right customers for the pilot is essential. If you do a pilot with a pure price buyer, you'll spend hours discussing prices. Value buyers or partnership seekers might show more patience.

Give credit. Of course everyone on your side and the customer side will be working hard on this effort. But there's an old saying that goes something like this: it's amazing what can get accomplished when no one worries about who gets the credit. We recommend that you let the customer team take credit for the work being done. Your own rewards, both tangible and intangible, ultimately derive from customer success. They'll come in due time.

Show goodwill. As in any other strategic project, not everything will work according to plan. Recall that you're exploring new avenues together with your customer. You're jointly co-creating your new digital offer; you're both in co-incubation mode. In such a context, it's inevitable that during rapid prototyping unforeseen hurdles emerge. To remove those roadblocks, be ready to absorb unexpected small expenses to keep your project on track. Your willingness to step in when needed will go a long way toward signaling to your customer that you're a trustworthy partner. Be prepared to include a small discretionary budget to be allocated to key pilot projects and experiments.

Bring your legal team only when needed. Finally, we have to discuss the role of your legal team, because you can't undertake a data monetization program as described in this book without taking into account all legal concerns. Your legal subject-matter experts should always be involved, but legal experts shouldn't drive the process. Piloting, testing, and scaling your offers requires speed and flexibility. If every change—and there will be many—requires a legal review, you'll not only kill goodwill. You may kill the entire project and, even worse, the customer relationship itself. You must be ready to make changes, be nimble, and absorb additional unexpected costs rather than subject every ongoing step to strict legal review. One final thought: think not only about whether and when to involve your legal experts but also about how to draw on their expertise. If you confront your legal team with very broad questions, such as "Can we take that level of risk in our future outcome-based contract?" you'll inevitably receive push-back from your legal team. But if you frame your question in a different way, your legal team can become your partner. For example, value propositions often require validation by your legal department: "Here's the data regarding value created, here are the cost improvements achieved when beta-testing our productivity service on our own equipment. From a legal perspective, can we make the following claim?" In other words, you need to onboard your legal experts, and you need to be clear about what you can ask them and what you cannot.

Preserving trust over time

Trust is a key relationship enabler that builds up over time. You must establish trust early on. But be aware that customers will monitor you throughout the project and search for confirmation that you are (and continue to be) trustworthy. You need to cultivate trust and maintain it, which requires ongoing efforts throughout the project. Failing to maintain trust can lead the customer to start restricting your access to data or delaying the process through cautious or overly protective behavior.

You could also experience the worst-case scenario. Let's say that you spend considerable time and money identifying and validating value, and the numbers are so compelling that the customer says, "Whoa! We should keep that for ourselves." They feel they can do the rest of the work on their own, because you've done such a thorough job educating them, giving them many parts of the solution, and showing them the robust roadmap.

What went wrong? What happened to the trust you worked so hard to build?

Leaving case-specific aspects aside, we can mention three approaches that can help you prevent this kind of outcome:

- **Always leave something to learn.** If you aren't careful, you can fall into what we call the customer university syndrome, which means that at some point the customer thinks they're teaching you more than you're teaching them. You mitigate this risk by having the customer feel that you're leading them through the process in a controlled fashion. This is why preparation and process management are important. You have a better idea of what will happen next, what could go wrong, and so forth, so they trust your judgment and need your input. The customer should always feel that they still have something important to learn from you.
- **Remind customers that the grass isn't greener elsewhere.** The customer should feel apprehensive about bringing in a different partner or going it alone. That feeling should not be a product of instilling fear on your part but rather of instilling trust and confidence derived from customer intimacy and demonstrating tangible results at each critical milestone of your project.
- **Caution customers against "easy" solutions.** This is where your internal validation of your own assets and your experience in other pilots become a huge asset. You're able to guide the customer through the process faster because you've experienced the pains yourself. You can credibly tell the customer when "two steps forward, one step back" is the best possible outcome in a certain situation, rather than a setback, because you've lived it and you know.

In sum, we saw in this chapter that mutual trust is paramount in any data monetization project. Customers must trust in your ability to achieve outcomes promised and feel confident in your motivation to work in both your and the customer's interest. You monitor the level of trust. Your best antidote to an erosion of trust is your own internal story. It will be very difficult to establish customer trust and to really hook your customers to do more work with you if you can't share your own internal experience. Telling the customer you've swallowed your own medicine enhances your credibility.

9

Step 6: Select and Execute the Right Pricing Model(s)

When you buy cloud or subscription software from a vendor, you can buy exactly how much you want: per person, per-employee, and pay as you go. It is a good business model and demand is strong, because everyone wants to buy software to make their companies efficient.

—Richard Davis, Canaccord Genuity

THROW THE SEARCH TERM *pricing* into Google and you will get over 500,000,000 hits. If you search under *subscription models* instead, you can narrow the pool of hits down to around 170,000,000. How can you sort and distill all that information into a useful set of tools and guidelines?

We take on that challenge for you in this chapter.

Regardless of your experience with pricing, with data-enabled offers, or with monetization, this chapter has many nuggets to offer you so that you can convince the key decision makers in your company to move away from cost-plus pricing. What makes the chapter unique is that we focus on real-world execution: how to prepare and make a good transition from one pricing model to another (usually from traditional to digital-based) and how to design complex pricing approaches or strategies that may require multiple models for different customer segments. The pricing novice will receive a straightforward, commonsense introduction to the basic tools and concepts and their applications. For those of you who are experienced in the pricing of digital offers, we explore new aspects of the change management required for developing and executing innovative pricing models. Either way, building these bridges for you was one of the primary inspirations for writing this book.

A reminder before we begin

Remember that a good pricing model design begins with a good business model design. In the end, though, the pricing model(s) you select will be the mechanism to capture value created. So the heart of the matter is the design of a relevant pricing model for your data-enabled offer within the context of a business model.

Before we get started, it's important to mention that the transition from an ownership business model to a usage-based or a performance-based business model isn't easy. This isn't just a pricing discussion. Changing your approach to pricing will inevitably affect many aspects of your business. As an illustration, here are some aspects to consider:

1 cannibalization of existing revenues
2 reduction of new equipment sales due to increased efficiencies or extended lifetime

3 cash-flow reduction during the transition phase
4 margin impact due to different pricing levels
5 incremental fixed costs to support new business models
6 impact on revenue recognition in accounting and taxes

Any transition from one business model to another will require deep discussions with business leaders about pricing decisions and an assessment of how to mitigate risks involved. Value-based pricing approaches and tools can become extremely beneficial at this stage. For example, conducting a new customer segmentation (as discussed in chapter 4) helps identify customers that are more opex- or capex-oriented. Segmentation also can help explain which customers are more risk averse than others. The dollarization process discussed earlier in this book is paramount when transitioning from one pricing approach to another. Finally, setting pricing must also include discussions about bundling, ramp-up pricing, and setting pricing guidelines. Ultimately, pricing can help manage the speed and the depth of the transition. There are risks, as you can see. So the pricing discussions will have to include both legal and risk management experts on your team. The discussions cannot happen in a vacuum.

The process begins with a customer value metric

The first critical task is to understand what value metric your customer has in mind. Your guidance here is the customer's language: How do key stakeholders speak about the problem(s) at hand? How do they describe the customer job(s) to be done? Do key customer stakeholders express expectations in terms of aircraft landings (e.g., tires), clicks obtained (e.g., online retailing), machine uptime (e.g., hydraulic pumps in power plants), or a pay-as-you-go metric (e.g., wafers produced in semiconductor manufacturing)? Gaining deep insights about KPIs that truly matter to customers is part of your journey to making better pricing decisions. Listening carefully to how customers describe what matters in their business environment and how they view success allows you to home in on a pricing model that is fully and naturally aligned with the customer. For example, if a customer constantly refers to cost savings, productivity gains, and asset efficiency optimization, you don't want to focus solely on an equipment price. Instead, you want to suggest a pricing approach that gives customers exactly what they need—not more, not less. We capture this idea in figure 9.1.

Once you know exactly which metrics the customer uses to express what they mean based on what jobs they're trying to do and how they go at it, the work begins on sharpening the metric or metrics. The metrics will need to be credible, compelling, and segment-specific. They also need to work hand in hand with the monetization approach you choose regarding data. Recall the breakdown of options we presented in chapter 1. You could decide to sell data, you could decide to incorporate the data into the product or as a module on top of the product, or you could decide to have a brand-new revenue model for your business based on data-enabled services. A combination of these options

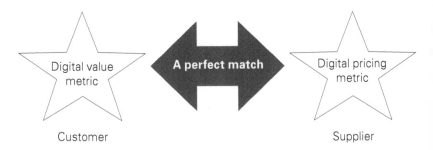

Figure 9.1. The perfect match begins with understanding the customer's language.

is also possible. In each case, the choice evokes an ideal pricing model and an accompanying metric.

As complex as the final construction of a pricing model may become, once you decide to move beyond a traditional pricing approach the model will ultimately fall into one of three categories: subscription-based, usage-based, or outcome-based pricing. This is why we've often used IoT and predictive maintenance as illustrative examples in the book so far. Figure 9.2 offers a high-level introduction to these interactions.

A legitimate question we hear often is whether it makes sense to innovate in pricing at all. People ask us why they can't just enter

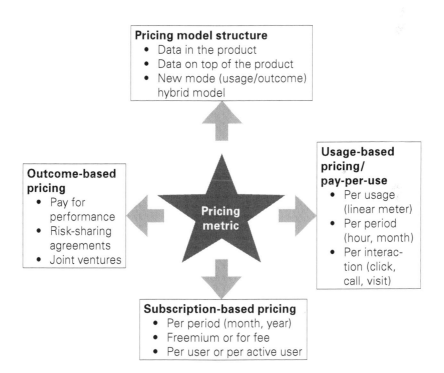

Figure 9.2. What you need to consider when choosing an optimal pricing metric.

into data-enabled services with a more traditional pricing metric. The answer always depends on the context, and ultimately on your business model. Let's look at this as a matter of degree. At one extreme, if you have a highly disruptive, strongly differentiated business model built around a unique value proposition for an offer that benefits from a large value pool and a high customer willingness to pay for your expertise and support in achieving cost savings and/or productivity gains, then the external conditions are ideal for introducing a new pricing metric. Note that changing a pricing metric may be considered a key competitive differentiator in its own right. For example, over many years, hospitals were accustomed to buying MRI scanners. When one medical device manufacturer changed its pricing approach, switching to leasing equipment instead of selling machines, it disrupted the market by setting a new standard. Competitors were taken by surprise. Over time, leasing MRI scanners became the new normal.

At the other extreme, consider situations where your offer's value pool is relatively limited, its value proposition lacks strong differentiation, and customers find it harder to see value created. Many traditional industries find themselves in such a context of rapid commoditization, such as construction or transportation. In such cases, you may need to stick with an existing pricing metric and a more traditional product formula with a module of services or data on top of your current product offering. But also many data-enabled offers face a growing risk of finding themselves under similar pressures. Given a lack of significant differentiation, the value pool of such offers is low. Here again, managers might carefully weigh the pros and cons of deviating from a more traditional pricing approach.

We're not trying to discourage innovation. Far from it! We're just being realistic about executing an innovative model, no matter how attractive it looks on paper. In a market where disruption is low, quick inundation is the path to seizing profit opportunity now. That often means forgoing an innovative model. During the time you'll spend trying to train your own salesforce, educate your customers, and then convince them to accept your innovative pricing model, your competitors will be making massive inroads into the market. Yes, you have to take risks, but sometimes a risk is a waste.

The factors involved in the decision process described in figure 9.3 are not exhaustive. But they give you a first set of criteria to help you to think through the pros and cons of introducing an innovative pricing approach in your industry—relative to competition. Speaking of competition, remember that your competition in the digital space also has the opportunity to innovate with its pricing models. Once one supplier has set the stage, you may have no other option than to follow suit and offer a different pricing model as well. If Deloitte Digital offers monthly subscriptions to an IoT platform, your customers and prospects might be asking for the same model.

(main text continues on page 180)

Business model and customer value proposition that are
- Disruptive
- Differentiating
- Solution-oriented
- High value pool
- High customer WTP

New pricing model to capture value using a **new** pricing metric as part of a **unique** profit formula (new pricing frame of reference versus competitors)

Business model and customer value proposition that are
- Incremental
- Quickly imitable
- Product-oriented
- Low value pool
- In traditional sector

New pricing model to capture value using an **existing** pricing metric as part of a **traditional** profit formula (premium versus competitors based on value)

Figure 9.3. The two basic options for generating digital pricing models.

Siemens's MindSphere Pricing Model

MindSphere is an open ecosystem using data from production assets and enabling customers to extract value from their data. Siemens establishes that MindSphere is a key differentiator for the company. MindSphere is a scalable infrastructure for collecting data from production assets and making them available to value-added analytics. MindSphere is low cost and allows SMEs to join the platform. The ecosystem is fully transparent, has a low cost of entry, and employs a convenient pricing model based on usage.

Siemens designed a unique pricing model and pricing currency (called MSU) for the IoT platform. The model is pay-per-use and has three components:[1]

1 Fixed fee for MindConnect (€990)
2 Monthly fees for licenses (€150 for 50 users + 30 MSU for additional user → €3 per license)
3 Pay-per-use for data model (using MSU)

The MindSphere currency is called the MindSphere Unit (MSU). Each MSU is worth €0.1 and is the basis for fees invoiced monthly. The sum of calculated MSU depends on

1 Number of **data points** (number of connected elements)
2 **Reading cycle** of a data point (every second, or every 15 seconds . . .)
3 **Data types** (Boolean is the lowest value and String is the highest value)

---

1   https://community.plm.automation.siemens.com/t5
     /MindSphere-FAQs/What-is-the-pricing-model-of-MindSphere
     /ta-p/403910

Let's look at an example of data point calculation:[2]

Asset	Data point	Reading cycle
Motor (x3)	1. Motor torque	1 min
	2. Motor speed	1 min
	3. Motor current	1 min
	4. Motor power	1 min
	5. DC link voltage	1 min
	6. Vibration RMS of the non-drive of the motor	1 min
	7. Vibration RMS of the drive end motor	1 min
Pump (x3)	1. Vibration RMS of pump bearings	1 min
Flowmeter (x1)	1. Flow rate data from the common flowmeter	1 min
Inverter (x1)	1. Inverter temperature (measured heat sink temperature)	1 min
	2. Inverter temperature (chip temperature)	1 min
	3. Inverter temperature (rectifier temperature)	1 min
	4. Inverter temperature (inverter ambient temperature)	1 min
	5. Inverter temperature (control board temperature)	1 min
	6. Fil. power factor	1 min
	7. Energy consumption meter	1 min

$$= (3 \times 7) + (3 \times 1) + (1 \times 1) + (1 \times 7) = \textbf{32 data points}$$

Price levels:

	MindConnect	User access	Application	Data model
Quantity	1 MCN	50 users	Fleet Manager = 150 MSU	32 data points = 32 MSU
Price	€990	€150	€15	€3.2
Frequency	one-off costs	per month		

---

2   https://community.plm.automation.siemens.com/t5
     /MindSphere-FAQs/What-is-the-pricing-model-of-MindSphere
     /ta-p/403910

(continued from page 177)

Choosing a pricing model: Four options

When a search on *pricing* returns hundreds of millions of Google hits, you can imagine the amount of noise and clutter to sort through. In our review of over 250 reports, we took a first pass at categorizing the various types of pricing models while also trying to ensure that we left no stone unturned. Each of the organizations we mention in figure 9.4 adds its own perspective to the range of available models. Collectively, they provide a good overview of the breadth and depth of options that companies can choose from for monetizing a data-enabled service offer. This is what the major consulting firms are discussing in the area of pricing today.

To keep things as simple as possible, we distill the available options even further. We identify four distinct models: a product pricing model, a subscription pricing model, a pay-per-use, and a performance-sharing or outcome-based model. We feel that these are intuitive, self-explanatory, and most applicable to an industrial B2B environment. In the rest of this chapter, we elaborate on each of these models before concluding with a thorough discussion of the implementation risks and challenges. The four models and their pros and cons are summarized in figure 9.5.

Once companies move toward growing beyond their traditional product core into services, and especially into data-enabled services, managers often find themselves faced with the challenge of giving away too much value. Wolfgang has developed a roadmap for helping managers transform services given away free of charge into services that are invoiced to customers, or transitioning services "from free to fee." One way to avoid this nagging problem from the outset is to carefully think about the right pricing model before launching your new data-based service offer.

It's often difficult to reflect high-value services in a product's price or in a rental or leasing model. But at the same time, small

Consulting firm/ publication	Data pricing model classification
Tech Product Management (2018)	• Subscription model • Outcome-based model • Asset-sharing model
BCG (2018)	• Subscription model • Pay-per-use model • Value-sharing model
Frost & Sullivan (2018)	• Bartering model (data-based exchanges) • Brokering model (data-based brokering) • Business intelligence model (data-based services)
Simon-Kucher & Partners (2018)	• Alternative metric • Subscription pricing model • Dynamic pricing • Auctions • Freemium model
ConnectedValue (2018)	• Purchase pricing model • Leasing and rental model • Pay-per-use pricing model • Pay-per-outcome pricing model
PA Consulting (2017)	• Product pricing model • Output pricing model • Outcome pricing model
Accenture (2016)	• Product pricing premium model • Pay-per-use model • Pay-per-outcome model
McKinsey (2015)	• Pay-per-usage model • Subscription-based model • Licensing model for data standards or software
Capgemini Consulting (2014)	• One-time charge model • Pay-for-results pricing model • Freemium model • Subscription model • Pay-as-you-go pricing model
Keystone (2014)	• Traditional/modular subscription • Sharing savings pricing model • Software licensing model

Figure 9.4. Different terminology, but similar underlying concepts.

	Product pricing model	Subscription model	Pay-per-use model	Performance-sharing model
Price metric	Premium in the product unit price	Pay per time interval for a set price	Pay for usage of the product	Pay for value created for the customer
Pros	• Stable • Known, so low risk • Easy to deploy • Liked by sales teams • High margins	• Recurring revenues • Versioning options • Quick innovation • Customer centric • Upselling opportunity	• Customer focused • Product closeness • Flexibility in rate • Low commitment • Opex focused	• Focused on jobs to be done • Focused on customer value • Skin in the game • Strong shared incentive • Forges strong relationships
Cons	• Cost centered • Low capture rate • Set on upfront fee • Undermines services • Lack of customer intimacy over time	• IT/ERP constraints • Cost to scaling • Lack of market access • Customer churn • Requires minimum level of retention • Easy to copy	• IT/ERP constraints • Financial risk • Tough transition period • Unpredictable usage • Less adapted to high usage account • Easy to copy	• Financial risk • Contract complexity • Customer loss of control • Requires operational predictability • Required customer intimacy • Difficulty in renewing once value is shared

Figure 9.5. The four main digital pricing models.

steps could spark a transition to value-based pricing and ultimately to more sophisticated models. This is especially true if your business has been traditionally cost-plus centered. If you can capture more value through better pricing of your offer, it could mark an additional step in your maturity development. Don't get us wrong. There are situations where selling a product, an integrated system, and added services is the right thing to do. However, in this chapter, we want to draw your attention to the fact that, by taking a step back, by reviewing all options on the table, you might spot a great opportunity for innovating in your market through a novel pricing approach, differentiating yourself from competition, and capturing more value than others. Pricing innovation will come to your industry at some point, even if you compete primarily with industrial natives. Some company will begin to carve out a competitive advantage based on an alternative pricing model, as Siemens did with MindSphere. If your competitors force you toward subscriptions or pay-per-use, how ready will you be? Will you be ready to manage a vast number of customers paying you a small monthly subscription fee? Are your ERP systems and customer fulfillment teams ready to handle all the additional work? Consider the example of Expensify, a B2B expense management platform created in 2008. By 2012 they had 100,000 users. By 2017 they had grown to 5 million users. You might be better off disrupting yourself than waiting it out and being disrupted by others when it's too late.

Product pricing model in detail

The product pricing model effectively treats data-enabled services as another important product feature or option, rather than as a powerful stand-alone revenue and profit source worthy of its own monetization model. While this is a straightforward pricing approach, we've seen many problems arise from this easy-to-understand method. Let's focus here on three of the most frequently met challenges we've seen when working with firms on services pricing. First, by recognizing a digital offer's added value as a "premium" on top of the product's price, managers frequently run into the problem of margin stacking. The overall price becomes so expensive that customers are reluctant to pay, especially where there is a significant difference between the product price and the service price. In such cases, customers expect to receive the digital offer for free, as icing on the cake. Second, we've repeatedly seen managers hide a value-adding digital service in an overall bundled price. But such decisions can equally upset customers. "Why should we pay for something we don't need?" is a frequent customer complaint. While such a managerial heuristic is understandable, it's often the wrong thing to do. The third approach we've seen is to abandon pricing the digital offer altogether in hope of selling more components, equipment, or systems in the long run. The problem with this approach is that it often translates to wishful thinking, rather than a proactive, strategic approach to pricing your offer in the market.

There are many ways to address these problems. You can create different bundles of services around your core products or offer services à la carte, with customers choosing from a menu. Rental or leasing models represent intermediary steps for capturing more value. Figure 9.6 lists these and other options.

We won't spend too much time on the traditional product model, despite its role as a fallback position as mentioned above. It can be an adequate approach, but you need to be aware of what you're giving up. The product model's advantages are that it is stable, low risk, and easily understood. Your organization is probably designed around such models. But these advantages are offset by the lost opportunity to expand your market. You also continue to

---

Product pricing models

1 Product price premium includes data and services
2 Product, services, and data are packaged in bundled offers
3 Components of offer are listed in à-la-carte pricing menu
4 Data and services are proposed as an add-on to product pricing
5 Product solution is leased or rented to customers

Figure 9.6. The types of product-based pricing models.

expose yourself to extensive negotiations with very professional buyers trained on that kind of model. Although you may still enjoy good margins, we don't recommend this approach, because of the intense dematerialization trends in the industrial digital economy. Competing solely on products is not sustainable in the long run. We suggest that you always try to bring innovation to all key building blocks of your digital business model—including pricing.

Subscription models in detail

Whether it's Netflix, a streaming music service, or a magazine, it's easy for most people to conceptualize and understand how subscription models work. Subscription models have been around a long time and take a variety of forms. As more industries transition from manufacturing to services, subscriptions are becoming an increasingly popular pricing model in B2B industrial goods as well. Figure 9.7 lists several of the more common and effective forms of subscriptions, along with their pros and cons.

Subscription models have several features in common, including the revenue model, the business opportunities, and the business challenges.

Subscription type	Description	Pros	Cons
Flat rate	Fee for a single product per month or per year	Easy to sell; easy to communicate; transparent	One size fits all; no flexibility; forgets heavy users
Pay-as-you-go	Fee directly related to the rate of usage	Price variability; lower barrier to use; addresses heavy users	Lack of value focus; too usage focused; unpredictable
Tiered pricing	Packages matching combinations of features at different price points	Linked to segmentation; value focused; upselling power	Less clear; too transparent on costs; risk of error in setup
Per user	Fee for number of users signed up	Simple; focused on adoption; predictable revenues	Makes churn easier; unfair for low users, limits adoption
Per active user	Fee for number of active users	More fair; favors retention; customer intimacy	Definition of active; converting rate issues
Per feature	Fee per feature or block of features	Versioning; upselling power; clearer	Perception of nit picking; difficult to get right
Freemium	Part of a tiered pricing strategy as an entry tier	Foot in the door; upselling power; scalability and virality	Churn rate; devalues IP; potential revenue killer

Figure 9.7. Types of subscription pricing models.

- **Revenue model.** The customer pays the supplier at regular intervals (e.g., monthly, quarterly, or annually) for a service or a bundle of products and services. This implies a transition to a monthly recurring revenue model. But it doesn't mean that the supplier needs to offer one fixed price (flat rate). The supplier can offer tiers of service at different rates, which makes sense because demand, willingness to pay, and so forth will vary by segment.

- **Business opportunities.** The secret of the subscription model lies in its power to generate deeper insights into customer usage patterns. This knowledge creates new opportunities for cross-selling and upselling (e.g., more usage, add-ons, new versions). It also offers suppliers a unique opportunity to innovate quickly and move customers to higher-priced options.
- **Business challenges.** If you offer subscriptions without a set contract duration, the customer can opt out at any time. This means that you need to focus constantly on delivering a steady stream of value, or using dynamic pricing, to retain subscribers. The transition to a subscription-based model can take time and be difficult. You need to evaluate the cash-flow implications during the transition because monthly payments are generally much smaller than upfront revenues generated in the form of a transactional product.

Subscription-based pricing models aren't new. They've been embraced in the software world for quite a while with the emergence of software-as-a-service (SaaS) models. What's new is that we're seeing industrial natives introduce new digital opportunities using subscriptions. Schneider Electric, Alcatel Lucent, BEA, Thales, GE, Renault, BAE, Caterpillar, and others are jumping into the subscription tsunami. Zuora, a leading player in this area, calls this the *subscription economy*. The company's recent introduction in the stock market shows that financial and stock analysts are paying attention to this new business model.

Pay-per-use models in detail

People also tend to understand the pay-per-use model implicitly, because we often pay for goods or services per click, per landing,

(*main text continues on page 190*)

The Subscription Economy, *by Zuora*

Komatsu: Dirt removal as a service

Subscription in the B2B world is becoming a reality, particularly for dirt, heavy equipment, and service-level agreements. Let's take a look at construction. One of the first steps in building something is figuring out how much dirt you need to dig in order to lay the foundation. Worksite surveying is a pretty inefficient process. Manual surveys generally have a 20 to 30 percent margin of error—that affects equipment rentals, material purchases, labor hiring, completion plans, everything. According to McKinsey, big construction projects routinely run up to 80 percent over budget, and typically take 20 percent longer to finish than the original completion plan. Surveys can also take several weeks to complete. Plus, information is routinely scattered across various blueprints and databases, making it much easier for mistakes to happen. All this is about to change.

Today Komatsu can finish a worksite survey in 30 minutes. Komatsu was founded in 1921 and is one of the world's oldest construction and mining equipment manufacturers. A couple of years ago it launched a new service, Smart Construction, that takes advantage of the same kind of new radar technology that's driving automobile automation in order to take the manual guesswork out of site surveying. When the Komatsu team arrives at your job site, the first thing they do is unleash a bunch of awesome-looking drones into the sky (they have some great videos on YouTube).

The drones create a 3D-rendered topographical model of your worksite in centimeter-level detail. Komatsu maps that 3D rendering to your worksite blueprint in order to calculate the exact area and volume of earth to be removed. Then, much like the artificial intelligence programs that people play chess against, they run thousands of simulations of possible scenarios within this new virtual worksite to determine the best possible approach. The result is a finished project plan, with materials, equipment, labor, and a work schedule detailed to the last hour.

The labor part is particularly interesting. At home in Japan, Komatsu is dealing with an aging workforce. Here in the US, there's strong manufacturing demand but a lack of qualified equipment managers. So Komatsu feeds your project plan into its fleet of semiautonomous excavators, bulldozers, and backhoes, and these giant robots basically take care of the project for you. In much the same way that the pilot of a 747 only "flies" her aircraft for seven to ten minutes per flight, your equipment managers are mostly there to supervise. And like something out of *Star Wars,* site managers can sit in front of their 3D virtual worksite, follow progress in real time (rotate, zoom in, zoom out, etc.), and run simulations for any plan changes they might want to consider.

So what's Zuora doing with Komatsu? The same thing we're doing with Caterpillar—we're helping them change the question from "How many trucks can I sell you?" to "How much dirt do you need moved?" By handling the subscription finances behind these services, we're helping to power dirt removal as a service.

Caterpillar: Services inside servers

Caterpillar recently came to our Subscribed conference to talk about how they're tackling the challenge of getting involved in customers' businesses even before there's a worksite. They're asking big questions about how they can analyze data from one project to another and even help customers win more business. Case in point: a couple of years ago Caterpillar was approached by a client with more than 16,000 pieces of equipment. They wanted to be able to manage each of those assets from a single screen: utilization, fuel amounts, idle time, and so on. Caterpillar retrofitted the entire fleet, and a year later the client reported an almost 20 percent utilization increase.

Caterpillar also manufactures giant mining trucks. They're ridiculously huge—the truck bed can hold more than 200 regular-size cars. The driver sits two and a half stories up in the air. They look like giant Tonka trucks, but they're essentially semiautonomous rolling factories. One of their clients had one breakdown in the field, and it cost them $650,000 and 900 hours of downtime.

Today Caterpillar offers an analytics platform, called Cat Connect Solutions, that lets site managers avoid such problems—or at least anticipate them. They can figure out when a machine needs servicing by monitoring things like vibration patterns and comparing them with the past usage data of identical machines. That helps them schedule at-risk machines into a maintenance session that could bring those numbers down to $12,000 and 24 hours of downtime. Now, that's an incredibly valuable service. And where did it come from? The information generated by Caterpillar's fleet.

Manufacturers and OEMs all over the world are waking up to the fact that there are dozens of potentially new value-added services sitting right inside their servers.

(*continued from page 187*)
per kilometer, and so forth. But on the supplier side, this model and outcome-based models both present a huge challenge in terms of risk management. You must access, collect, and track usage data. You also must understand who has the rights to the data. Figure 9.8 shows the prerequisites for developing and implementing a pay-per-use model.

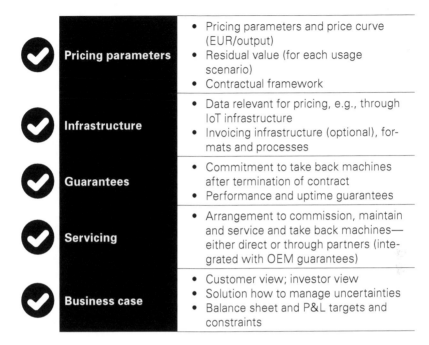

✓	**Pricing parameters**	• Pricing parameters and price curve (EUR/output) • Residual value (for each usage scenario) • Contractual framework
✓	**Infrastructure**	• Data relevant for pricing, e.g., through IoT infrastructure • Invoicing infrastructure (optional), formats and processes
✓	**Guarantees**	• Commitment to take back machines after termination of contract • Performance and uptime guarantees
✓	**Servicing**	• Arrangement to commission, maintain and service and take back machines—either direct or through partners (integrated with OEM guarantees)
✓	**Business case**	• Customer view; investor view • Solution how to manage uncertainties • Balance sheet and P&L targets and constraints

Figure 9.8. The prerequisites for a pay-per-use model (courtesy of ConnectedValue).

Pay-per-use likewise presents significant challenges, many of which stem from the fact that this revenue model, compared with subscriptions, is a more volatile replacement for the traditional product model of upfront purchases. The entire structure of a company's revenue inflows changes, with repercussions for its sales, support, and distribution networks, all of which were originally conceived and optimized for upfront purchases.

One potential downside of pay-per-use models is cannibalization of underlying product sales. For example, when a truck fleet operator changes from buying tires to paying a tire manufacturer based on number of miles rolled per month, efficient and effective use of tires within a fleet management contract may result in a significant decrease in the number of tires needed to get the job done. A second potential challenge lies in favoring a perception among customers that offers are increasingly commoditized. For example, once customers learned that they could pay per copy instead of buying photocopying machines, it became easier to compare suppliers with each other and shop for the lowest-price bidder. Third, the model can also come as a shock to existing customers who made an upfront purchase—and the associated large financial outlays—only to see a competitor receive a potential financial advantage with the pay-per-use model. At the same time, customers who invested heavily upfront in equipment may be harder to acquire than pay-per-use customers because of high switching costs.

It may be difficult for sales teams to change their mindset from a practice of selling complex expensive goods and/or systems to customers to a practice of selling services and customer solutions, often in the form of multiyear contractual agreements (see Wolfgang's research on transforming the salesforce from a product-centric to a service-savvy model[11]). Compounding this is the wide range of offerings and contracts at different prices using different pricing models. Finally, a company may not be able to handle a larger number of customers resulting from the pay-per-use model or to address the changes in cash flow due to a lack of financial strength.

By no means are we trying to discourage you from considering or adopting this kind of model. Many companies have successfully adopted them, as figure 9.9 shows. What we want to ensure is that you carefully consider all the financial, cultural, and commercial factors before making the transition.

(*main text continues on page 198*)

---

11   Wolfgang Ulaga and James Loveland, "Transitioning from Product to Service-Led Growth in Manufacturing Firms: Emergent Challenges in Selecting and Managing the Industrial Sales Force," *Industrial Marketing Management* 43 (January 2014): 113–25.

Equipment-as-a-Service, *by ConnectedValue*

New machines and new equipment no longer operate in isolation, as previous generations of machines did. They're connected and integrated. While the opportunities of the Industrial Internet of Things or the Digital Industry are broadly discussed and part of every management agenda, the strategic implications for business, pricing, and refinancing models are often neglected or unclear. Business and pricing models will change fundamentally into value-based equipment-as-a-service (EaaS) offerings.

Value-creating solutions require appropriate ways to capture, guarantee, and distribute value. Providing customer-centric solutions means creating value not only by managing and optimizing a single machine but also by improving the processes and operations supported by the machine. The center of value creation is shifting away from "keeping the machinery running" to optimizing assets, processes, operations, and even businesses. But how can new value creation be shared between the OEM and the industrial user? Selling or renting the equipment does not fully account for the full value created. Let's assume that you double the productivity of your machine by optimizing workflow, utilization, or lifetime. Aren't you running the risk of losing sales revenue? Depending on the value you create, business and pricing models must shift from selling and renting to pay-per-use, pay-per-output, pay-per-savings, or even pay-per-result models.

What do equipment-as-a-service business models look like?

To explain the principles of value-based pricing solutions, consider new "agricultural-equipment-as-a-service" offerings, also known as digital farming. Autonomous vehicles might

optimize seeds and other consumables, for example fertiliz-
ers, pesticides, and herbicides. If you ask farmers why they
don't invest in this vision you typically get three answers: (1)
uncertainty about the results or return, (2) high investment
costs with all the risks allocated to the user, and (3) incompatible and poor interoperability of technology.

The first two issues, the (1) uncertain return on investment
and (2) high investment costs, are addressed by the "equipment as a service" package visualized in figure 9C1. Instead
of the machinery being bought or rented, its use is invoiced
based on the uptime or hectares of cultivated agricultural
land. All spare parts, consumables, and services are included.
One OEM goes so far as to guarantee the fuel consumption
because its tractors are more efficient than those of competitors. This is a key differentiator, as fuel consumption is a
significant factor from a life-cycle perspective in operating the
tractor. Important value levers are productivity, fuel consumption, maintenance, utilization, and durability. If additional value
is created, both groups, OEMs and farmers, benefit.

The second solution goes one step further and addresses
the third concern of farmers: the compatibility and interoperability of technology and the "right" configuration. Based
on the farm characteristics (size, production, livestock, etc.)
the company helps the farmer configure the optimal equipment portfolio. Pricing is based on the use or quantity, and
quality of the land. As a result, the costs are very predictable
to the farmer.

But some benefits of new agricultural technologies are
rooted in the efficiency of the use of seeds, herbicides,
pesticides, and so forth and improved harvest productivity.
The value generation may even be higher than for those on
the operational side. Ultimately the agricultural trading company (with the manufacturer of the equipment) can provide
some guarantees on the amount with respect to costs of the

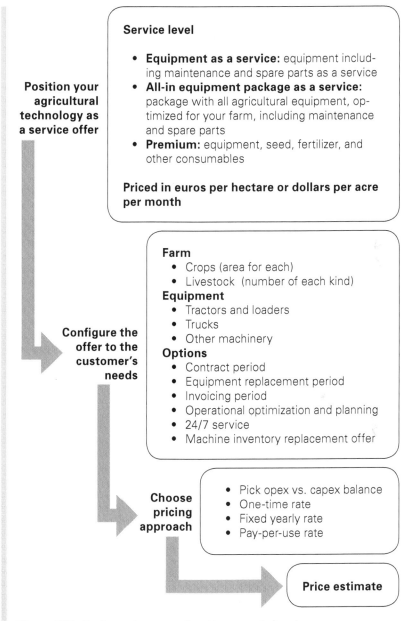

Position your agricultural technology as a service offer

Service level

- **Equipment as a service:** equipment including maintenance and spare parts as a service
- **All-in equipment package as a service:** package with all agricultural equipment, optimized for your farm, including maintenance and spare parts
- **Premium:** equipment, seed, fertilizer, and other consumables

Priced in euros per hectare or dollars per acre per month

Configure the offer to the customer's needs

Farm
- Crops (area for each)
- Livestock (number of each kind)

Equipment
- Tractors and loaders
- Trucks
- Other machinery

Options
- Contract period
- Equipment replacement period
- Invoicing period
- Operational optimization and planning
- 24/7 service
- Machine inventory replacement offer

Choose pricing approach

- Pick opex vs. capex balance
- One-time rate
- Fixed yearly rate
- Pay-per-use rate

Price estimate

Figure 9C1. Equipment as a service. Use case 1: farming.

seeds, herbicides, and so on, leveraging performance data, knowledge of the technology, and their trading know-how (premium solution). After all, one of the promises of digital farming is increased productivity.

How does equipment-as-a-service work?

Let's consider a manufacturer of industrial printing machines that are sold as complete production lines. The company has introduced a pay-per-imprint model for their machines including consumables (paint, finishing) based on the historical machine and consumption date. There are two reasons for this.

The manufacturer has developed a productivity solution that can significantly increase the output per machine (with fewer people) by integrating the printing process end-to-end and by optimizing the job management. The aggregated cost of (mostly third-party) consumables is higher than the machine value and can also be optimized.

Starting the first successful pay-per-use pilots is a great achievement. But how can a manufacturer scale its offering? There are some critical aspects of scaling:

- Pricing needs to be optimized and the piloted solutions transferred to new customers and solutions. If prices are calculated too conservatively and with a very short amortization period, this will attract bad risks, leading to a vicious cycle of higher costs, higher prices, and even worse customer selection.
- "True sales" need to be realized, and therefore a flexible refinancing solution to avoid inflating the balance sheet and to protect the current P&L is required. The OEM might also pass on some volatility, for example, the flexibility of the payments made by the users.

- Finally, invoicing is different for a selling or a rental model with a fixed amount to be paid every month. In the piloting phase, it's okay to be pragmatic. But if equipment-as-a-service becomes an important part of the business and external refinancing is involved, a robust and auditable invoicing solution should be installed, while avoiding the start of a large IT project.

Figure 9C2 illustrates a pay-per-use case study. In a nutshell, we are adding to the product and connectivity layer of the manufacturer a pay-per-use pricing and refinancing layer. The usage and machine data from the connectivity solution is transformed into invoicing and converted back into the ERP system.

Step	Manufacturer		ConnectedValue
1	Generates usage and other metrics on hardware, materials, service offerings, sourcing	→	Creates diagnostics for cost, risk, and value
2	Automatically reports and summarizes data	→	Creates inventory of data, assesses its fitness relative to requirements for invoicing and refinancing
3	Defines pricing models (solution bundle, pay-per-use)	→	Formats and processes invoices, creates digital bridge to ERP system
4	Maintains financial structure	→	Conducts investor testing, financial reporting, investor matching, securitization

Figure 9C2. How to scale an equipment-as-a-service business offering. Use case 2: offset printing.

Company/ products	From	To
Hilti commercial tools	Price per tool	Monthly leasing fee or price per hole
Michelin aircraft tire	Price per tire	Price per landing
GE engines	Price per engine	Price per mile
Thales drones	Price per drone	Price per hour of operations
Schindler Industries	Price per elevator system	Price per distance and per transported passenger
BASF coatings	Price per kg of paints	Price per painted car
Michelin Truck Solutions	Price per tire	Price per mile
Microsoft 365	Price per license	Monthly subscription per user
SKF	Price per product	Price per product plus shared savings

Figure 9.9. Examples of pay-per-use models.

(continued from page 192)

There are many situations where a pay-per-use model can make sense:

- **Your solution allows customers to gain more value.** Pay-per-use models allow customers to derive more value from your offer combining goods, expertise, and deep knowledge of customer applications. For example, by buying and managing tires on their own, truck fleet operators often fail to extract the full value creation potential. A pay-per-mile fleet management contract allows customers to achieve more productivity gains and cost savings.
- **Customers lack sufficient investment budgets.** Pay-per-use may help convince your customer to switch from

a capex model to an opex model, which allows them to pay for your offer over time by avoiding initial upfront investments. For example, public universities can replace outdated air-conditioning systems with state-of-the-art alternatives by financing such projects through multiyear contracts guaranteeing energy cost savings.

- **You have a large untapped market.** If only a small number of customers can afford your solution right now, a less capex-oriented model may allow many more customers to afford your solution, because you've completely changed your pricing metric. For example, hospitals can access more sophisticated diagnostics equipment using a pay-per-test model rather than acquiring the medical device.

- **Demand is cyclical or volatile, or usage tends to be low.** Customers might use your offer only at certain times, or they might have a tough time reliably forecasting their demand. Those factors may reduce your customers' willingness to pay a large upfront sum but make a pay-per-use model more reasonable. You remove a big item from a customer's list of objections. For example, warehouse operators can secure additional forklift truck capacity to cover spikes in demand with a pay-per-use model.

- **Short life cycles.** Rapid obsolescence or a fast replacement cycle is a huge detriment to heavy investment, and conversely a strong incentive for pay-per-use. You'll have to factor this in to your pricing model. While you want to give customers a state-of-the-art solution at all times, you don't want to continually give away upgrades at prices that are too low.

We summarize these points in figure 9.10. In short, pay-per-use makes your offer more affordable to more customers, but you need to absorb the risk of wider variance and forms of cash inflows.

> **Optimal conditions to use pay-per-use pricing models**
>
> - The product is very **expensive**
> - The **customer pool** can be dramatically expanded with lower-priced offers
> - Low **product utilization** in the customer process
> - The customer experiences very volatile and **unpredictable** demand cycles
> - Fast product **obsolescence** rate with short product life cycles

Figure 9.10. Optimal conditions for pay-per-use models.

Outcome-based models in detail

The move from pay-per-use to outcome-based pricing isn't easy. The concept, though, is simple. You get paid for the outcome you deliver to customers. But this model requires incredibly thorough preparation. It's the most advanced pricing model of all and perhaps the most compelling, especially when you're trying to

(main text continues on page 204)

Outcome-Based Model:
The Enlighted Inc.'s GEO Case Study

Enlighted Inc. (a Siemens company) offers the only lighting-as-a-service, cloud-based intelligent sensor system in the world. It is fully hosted software for lighting savings and real-time visibility across the customer's real estate portfolio with 24/7 access from any browser. GEO (Global Energy Optimization) is a disruptive business model that allows customers to improve facilities without upfront capital spending and without exposing themselves to risk. GEO offers tremendous customer benefits in the area of solution deployment and operational savings. GEO's tangible benefits are listed on the company website as follows:

- Enlighted owns and maintains the lighting and intelligent system throughout the agreement.
- Enlighted maintains the software and provides upgrades to the lighting application.
- No debt or capital costs; payments are an operating expense.
- Energy savings offset all operating costs, resulting in net P&L benefits.
- Enlighted offers system performance guarantee; if system performs below expectations, Enlighted will make customer's payment obligations.

Enlighted's smart-lighting solution for commercial buildings delivers proven and guaranteed energy savings (often measured in hundreds of thousands of dollars per year, according to the case studies posted on their website). Besides direct operational savings, the GEO system can be used for things like determining traffic flow inside buildings and generating more efficient paths for workers moving around large warehouses all day. Enlighted lists an impressive array of clients, including Geodis, AT&T, Interface, JDS Uniphase, Amazon, HP, and Google. For some of those clients, Enlighted has transformed the pricing model from an upfront acquisition model to an outcome-based pricing model.

The company faced two major issues in selling their revolutionary solution: upfront costs making large investments difficult in times of cash constraint, and challenges of integrating it into existing environments.

The company designed a unique and innovative business model in GEO. It involves purchasing/financing energy credits from utilities via financial institutions and then essentially offering products to their customers at no cost, with the promise of receiving a portion of the energy savings that their customers generate. The company positioned GEO versus

	Company 1 typical capital purchase	Company 2 GEO rollout
Year started	2010	2013
Love the product—70% savings	Yes	Yes
Buildings	11	201
Square feet	550K	20M
Paid	$1M as capital expense	$0 to GEO
Energy saving per year	$170K	$8M
100% adoption	100 years	3 years

Figure 9D1. GEO versus a capex project.

a traditional upfront capex acquisition model and not versus other potential competing systems. They compared both solutions on some of the most standard variables, as shown in figure 9D1.

The GEO outcome-based pricing model is solely based on lighting utility operational savings for a period of seven years. The model is displayed in figure 9D2.

What do we learn from this example?

1 It's essential to have access to the base year and to evaluate the as-is total cost.
2 The length of the performance-sharing agreement is capped at seven years. Any additional long-term savings are given to customers. This provides a tremendous incentive for customers to pay more during the first seven years.
3 Keep the model simple by focusing on one of the most compelling operational cost drivers: lighting energy costs.

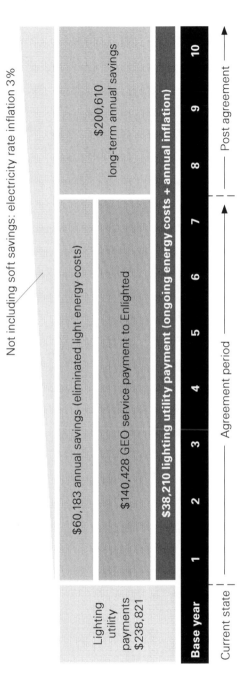

Figure 9D2. GEO's performance-based pricing model (adapted with permission from Enlighted Inc.).

4 Focus on the accelerated conversion rate thanks to the zero upfront payment. That drives the dramatic value/savings number.

5 All risks and upfront costs are absorbed by Enlighted Inc.

Visuals and data extracted from Enlighted Inc.'s website on May 11, 2018. GEO and Enlighted are property of Enlighted Inc.

(*continued from page 200*)
differentiate yourself from competition or you're trying to convince new customers to switch to a new business model.

At the same time, this model is the riskiest and demands very deep customer intimacy. It's not for everyone, and it might not be what you begin with when first growing the portfolio of your digital offers. This is a high-risk, high-payback model. It may take you a year or more to establish an outcome-based-pricing framework. You have to manage an outcome-based model very systematically. Nothing can be open to interpretation, which means you must make every effort to quantify and scale every aspect of the business model underlying such a pricing approach. To help facilitate and manage the process, we suggest ten steps for developing and implementing an outcome-based pricing model:

1 **Define the key objectives.** You need to invest time upfront to define your objectives. This means exchanging all relevant information and creating deep alignment with each individual customer, as each customer is different. You can't design such an offer on your own behind closed doors; you must do this jointly with the customer.

2 **Define the complete scope of negotiation.** You need to cover all elements and components of this joint effort: hardware, software, service components, tools, methods,

resources, experts, etc. This is an all-encompassing approach, so it's hard to go back and account for something you forgot upfront.

3 **Explore the wide range of possible outcomes.** Obviously you can't have outcome-based pricing without knowing what outcomes could serve as the basis. Then you need to understand all elements and components that directly impact the performance of your solutions.

4 **Reach agreement on what's controllable and what's not.** You need to discuss asset operational performance holistically (facilities, utilities, infrastructure, assets, software, data, IT, etc.), then reach agreement on

- what's controllable and what's not
- what's acceptable for outcome and what's not
- what will be included and excluded in your model/contract.

Every asset must be examined. You must understand, for example, whether certain assets are at risk of jeopardizing or adversely influencing the achievement of an outcome.

5 **Negotiate completely with a focus on past performance.** You need to recreate the past using real data if possible, and then project the impact of the solution and negotiate all aspects of a potential outcome. This is time-consuming but essential, because the past is exactly what you're going to do in the future, adjusted for variations due to human behavior, breakdowns in equipment, and so forth.

6 **Jointly develop clear measures and KPIs of achievement for each objective.** Together with the customer, you must define what performance means, how to calculate it, who calculates it, and what sources of data will be used. You may have to define new outcomes and jointly agree on metrics that must then be formalized in an agreement.

7 **Define explicit formulas to relate payment price to performance outcomes.** Payment amounts must be

defined precisely and unequivocally using a predefined functional relationship. This can also include how and when you'll be paid.

8 **Negotiate risk-reward penalties and adjustment formulas.** You have to prepare for variation and have rewards and penalties depending on the source of the variation. You can also include escalation or de-escalation formulas to automatically account for variations, especially for variation beyond each party's control.

9 **Specify a steering committee and mechanisms to resolve disagreements.** Despite the best of intentions, disputes can arise. Put in place a joint steering committee including members from both sides. Define and agree with your customers in advance what mechanisms you will use to arbitrate, mediate, or otherwise resolve a dispute.

10 **Define quarterly value verification audits.** This enables both parties to monitor and review the documented performance delivery. Are you delivering more or less than anticipated? Why? What adjustments may be necessary, and should provisions kick in?

As we mentioned, this is a high-risk, high-reward context. The risks fall into four categories: customer commitment, customer noncompliance, incorrect or incomplete assumptions, and failure to deliver (due to nonperformance, catastrophes, or force majeure).

- **Customer commitment.** One risk to consider is the long-term commitment of your customer, so that you can recover your own heavy investment over time and earn a profit. Payback periods could run as long as 20 years, so you must make sure the customer is a reliable long-term partner before you commit. Toward this end, you need to assess your customer's stability and try to predict potential variations in key stakeholders' behavior. Do they frequently switch suppliers, or do they act like partners? Do they have an established commitment to customer excellence, with the associated processes, or do they seem inconsistent?

- **Customer noncompliance.** Another risk, regardless of the general long-term orientation of your partner, is noncompliance. What happens if they don't follow operational recommendations or show no concern for costs? What if individual teams have different or conflicting agendas? You need a way to monitor compliance in terms of resources provided, activities performed, and so on. You'll need to develop the skills and tools for comprehensive risk assessment, complemented with what-if comparisons and exit plans. If there's a lot of operational variation or noncompliance, you need a way to exit the agreement.

- **Incorrect or incomplete assumptions.** Even if you've meticulously recreated the past for two years, there may still be factors that you and your customer didn't account for. In such cases, you'll need some flexibility in the contract. You should have periodic meetings for renewals at which you can discuss and review assumptions and conditions. This is especially urgent in the first 6 to 12 months of the agreement, before variation gets so far out of hand that you have an irreparable loss.

- **Failure to deliver (due to nonperformance, catastrophes, or force majeure).** You'll need to assess the reputational and financial risk of failing to deliver promised outcomes. Likewise, you'll need to assess any gains or excessive costs linked to unexpected or extreme events. Let's say that some catastrophic event generates additional costs of $1 million. Who absorbs the hit? What if there's a fire at the plant, a strike that prevents delivery, or a natural disaster? What insurance do you have lined up?

In some cases, you can use incentives or penalties to guide behavior. With enough experience, you can also implement guaranteed payments or minimum thresholds. The incentives—such as special fees, surcharges, or personalized pricing—can shape and reinforce customer behaviors in operations. You need to have some leeway or license to extract more from the sharing agreement, no matter whether the variation is intentional on the part of the customer or the result of legitimate experimentation. With increased maturity, you can introduce performance guarantees or minimum savings levels, supported by full or partial reimbursements. It may take years to reach this level, and if the relationship works unexpectedly in your favor, you need to decide how transparent you want to be with customers if it yields savings or efficiencies for you, outside the scope of the contract.

In many business markets, vendors have shifted partially or completely to outcome-based pricing, as shown in figure 9.11. One industry in which such pricing models gain traction fast is precision agriculture, where you have smart seeds, drones flying over land and informing farmers about humidity and soil quality, and analytics to predict crop yields based on data. There are two types of models for outcome-based pricing. In the first type of model, you take over an entire customer process or a portion of that process. The second type is where the customer and vendor

---

Industries/sectors using outcome-based pricing

- Precision agriculture
- IT outsourcing
- Supply chain services
- Marketing and advertising
- Health care
- Legal services
- Consulting services
- Power and utility
- Oil and gas
- Insurance

Figure 9.11. Examples of outcome-based pricing.

become so intertwined that a joint venture makes sense; in other words, the two parties create a separate entity to share the profit.[12]

Managing the transition

Selecting a pricing model and transitioning from one to the other when needed is not an easy task. Customers may have become used to a particular pricing model. They may have built their own expectations, planning processes, and structures around it. You're already operating in a certain set of constraints and processes, and in many industrial companies, processes are the operations bible. You can't tell a customer overnight that you're no longer relying on an established pricing approach. You can't force your customers to accept performance-based contracts if there's no appetite for them when it comes time to cut a large performance check. You need to have a plan B in place as well.

In most cases a B2B industrial company will be transitioning from a transactional pricing model (top left of figure 9.12) to a new digital pricing model (top right). The complexity in the selection and the design of pricing models lies in the integration (bottom of figure). Imagine that you have 20 MVPs coming out of your incubators over a period of three years, all having different pricing models with multiple value metrics. You still need to manage the back end. You need to validate and justify your value to your customers.

So the complexity lies less in the design of the pricing model itself, which is rather straightforward, especially with the help of a consultant. It instead lies in the integration, which is where the

(*main text continues on page 213*)

---

12   On invested relationships, see Kate Vitasek, Jeanette Nyden, Ed Hansen, and Astrid Uka, *Unpacking Pricing Models: Make "You Get What You Pay For" Real for Business Relationships* (University of Tennessee, Center for Executive Education, 2013).

Performance-Based Pricing Models in Practice, *by Experts in Value*

Even though **full performance-based pricing** is an ideal for both buyer and supplier, it's not always feasible. In theory, it makes a lot of sense for both the buyer and the seller to be in a win-win relationship: the buyer pays for only incremental economic value; the seller earns more than it can by selling a product alone because it delivers demonstrable tangible economic value. The reality is often a different story. Consider the following points:

- The buyer pays for outcomes and results for products and activities that *might* deliver value. Many limiting variables exist: the supplier needs other suppliers to reach full performance; the buyer needs to do things for value to be created; the operational risks are perceived as too high; the risks outweigh the rewards in the value calculation.
- Buying organizations might only be willing to outsource to experts *noncore* processes or services and are reluctant, for many reasons, to outsource their core activities. The end result is that the value numbers do not justify the complexity of performance-based contracts.
- The performance metrics are too dependent on the supplier's ability to educate the buying organization's staff in operations, in supply chain, or in administrative activities. If users must change their mindsets about how to conduct daily activities, it might take time to see the full benefits of an innovation. It's possible that machine operators will veer away from the recommended machine operating parameters and improvise to simplify their daily work.
- The buyer might conceptually be interested in a performance-based model but might not be able to get internal approval for a large cash outlay when it's time for

the CFO to cut checks! When the reward for great outcome reaches millions of dollars to be paid to suppliers, cash payments need to be approved by the C-suite or at the board level. Even if you can save a company $50 million over five years, it will be complicated to get the CEO/CFO to cut a check for $5 million or $10 million when all is said and done.

So there are economic, behavioral, and psychological barriers to performance-based agreements. It makes sense to propose these agreements to buying organizations along with other options. Discussing performance-based model(s) is a good idea as long as you have a plan B prepared that optimizes your value-capture potential. This plan B is often a **hybrid option** that seems the most palatable from the supplier's and buyer's perspectives. In this scenario, some risk and reward are added to the agreement on top of other pricing mechanisms. For the right customers, savings guarantees are exchanged with a position as a primary supplier and a higher price premium versus other suppliers. Value delivery is tracked by both parties after reaching approval on how value is calculated and what metrics are to be used. Risk and reward thresholds are then used to automatically increase or decrease price and share-of-wallet while maintaining a superior premium.

This hybrid product-premium/performance model is more acceptable to traditional and cash-sensitive buying organizations. There is still a need to conduct value-selling and education activities to convince stakeholders to pay larger premiums based on outcome and performance. For example, a 5 percent reduction in operating expenses is worth much more in financial terms than a 5 percent premium!

A last thought to consider is that the right pricing model to use depends somewhat on where the customer stands in the buying cycle. If the customer is at the needs-identification stage, this is a great time to frame the result they should be seeking when buying a solution and to discuss how best to align a contracting/pricing model to their needs. Are they buying bearings, belts, and sprockets, or are they buying parts that make their operations run at the best cost per ton of steel produced? In the early discovery stage, there's an opportunity to convince end users to pay on performance. If the RFP is issued, the customer has already decided on the purchasing characteristics and the weighting mechanism they will use to evaluate and select suppliers. In the latter stage the hybrid option might be more feasible. The customer is still buying parts at a higher price while getting a guarantee that the value created is worth much more than the price premium.

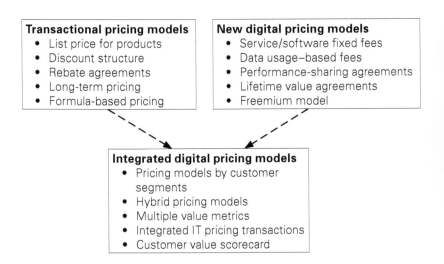

Figure 9.12. Hybrid model.

(continued from page 209)
process typically breaks down. The most frightening situations we've seen involve poorly prepared contracts that either ignore or incompletely consider the principles of risk management discussed in this chapter. Potential errors are too numerous to list, but the disastrous outcomes are always the same: either you're stuck with a contract where you're losing large amounts of money, or you're destroying your reputation. Both outcomes can be prevented if you're willing to do the homework. Figure 9.13 outlines the key issues.

Success in data monetization is all about integration, preparation, and managing complexity. This is where you have an opportunity to differentiate, especially in the industrial world, where even traditional pricing models often suffer from antiquated processes and suboptimal execution. Your company's reputation and credibility are at stake. If you go to a customer unprepared and

---

Innovation in pricing models requires preparation

- **Risk modeling**: financial, IP, operational, commercial
- **Financial implications** to the P&L during transition
- **Cannibalization** effect between old and new pricing model
- **Impact analysis** on existing contracts and relationship with traditional partners (distributors, resellers, etc.)
- Intense **customer education**: usage, rates, fees, behaviors
- Preparation of groundwork in IT and ERP **systems**
- Communication of **business rules** and new commercial conditions
- A review of commercial **contract** templates
- A review of roles, job descriptions, and incentives of the **salesforce**
- Talent review and hiring of **new talent** (from services, software, PaaS model, startups)

Figure 9.13. Success in data monetization is all about integration and preparation.

tell them "We want to do pay-per-use," you can't return three months later and say "Oops! We're sorry to return to our old pricing approach!" You'll lose customer trust. Here are eight factors critical to avoiding such blunders:

- **Risk modeling.** You must model not only on pilots but also on how you'll transfer intellectual property to customers, your operational side, and your commercial side. Can you actually retrieve data from customers' assets so you can analyze it? Can you collect data over time? To this end, you'll have to maintain the relationship over many years—with all the changes on both sides.

- **Financial implications.** You need a provisional profit-loss statement during the transition. You can't simply flip one of your MVPs from a capex to an opex model. You have to know how to recoup your investment. There are many financial details behind these decisions.

- **Cannibalization and impact analysis.** What happens to customers who are already buying your products? Announcing an abrupt switch of pricing models will scare the daylights out of customers and your sales team, regardless of the actual commercial and financial implications. You have to understand these potential effects up front.

- **Customer education.** Don't think that all customers will accept a switch from one pricing model to another one or to a hybrid one! Transitioning between models will require considerable efforts in customer education. Think of it this way. You save a customer $100 million, and your contract calls for you to receive $40 million as a result. What customer will write you a check for $40 million just like that? None! Customers don't like to write big checks to suppliers. This is a huge psychological barrier to implementing outcome-based models. In some cases, such payments have financial, cultural, fiduciary, or even legal implications.

- **IT and ERP groundwork.** The preliminary groundwork in IT and ERP cannot be underestimated. It's enormous, and it must begin immediately and continue intensively. How do you interconnect your own systems, never mind building the interfaces with customers? The change can be overwhelming.

- **Communication.** Your business rules, commercial conditions, and rules of engagement will change considerably. You have to make it clear that in the digital space, you're delivering solutions and outcomes, not (only) physical components and systems requiring different behaviors and modes of delivery.

- **Contracts.** You have to examine all your contracts, and all your business documents (including invoices), and then modify them for your digital offers. This means new contract templates.

- **Roles, responsibilities, and talent.** Your salespeople may now need to sell to customers under all four pricing models. Can they do that? How will you change their job description? How will you change the territory allocation and the sales distribution between the new and the old models? How will you incentivize them when they used to sell millions of dollars of hardware, but now they sell, say, subscriptions in $50,000 increments? How will you support them with training? Will you have single or specialized salesforces? You may need a larger or different talent pool for sales execution.

Then there is the full organizational structure. Do your data monetization activities take place within a separate company, or will you integrate all these digital business initiatives and their respective models into your core? These are C-level and board-level decisions.

Eight considerations when thinking about pricing model transition

Taking a deep dive into alternative pricing approaches, evaluating and selecting the right pricing model for your digital offer raises many fundamental issues. To summarize our discussion in this chapter, we want to highlight eight strategic pricing issues you must consider:

1 **Name a digital pricing champion.** If you don't have a dedicated pricing team managing core business pricing decisions today, who will manage the transition from the existing pricing model to the new model(s)? For example, if you're selling perpetual software licenses, how fast do you move toward a SaaS business model? How aggressive in pricing do you want to be to change customer behaviors? How do you price dual solutions for a period of two years? Someone at your company needs to steer the process of answering these questions.

2 **Embrace the 3 C's for setting prices.** Most B2B companies use cost-based or competitor-based pricing when setting prices. New pricing models need to embrace the 3 C's of pricing (cost, competition, customer) to inform your digital pricing decision. Once you've identified the right data from your 3 C's, what's the right price level? If you have a complex pricing structure (upfront + subscription + PPU), who designs the right mix and the right pricing levels? How do you test this mix?

3 **Reduce complexity of subscription-based pricing.** It's not all about freemium and then you're done! You have to manage handling collection, handling churn and subscription changes, measuring impact of subscription changes, revenue recognition including managing subscription changes, and

order management related to changes in subscription. Can your operational back office and your IT systems manage all of this?

4 **Manage change.** New pricing models mean different potential headaches internally and externally. We know the grass is always greener on the other side, but are you ready to educate your sales teams and your customer about the new pricing model? Have you considered all the back-office implications? Most importantly, how will you address resistance to change, both from your customers and within your own organization?

5 **Keep your eyes on competition.** Changing your pricing model does not shield you from competitive pressure. Continuous differentiation is still needed to maintain price premiums and sustainable sales performance. You might have made the switch to a subscription-based pricing model. Great work. Your competitors might also make this change a few months later. What do you do next? Changing the pricing model is critical, but it's not the heart of the matter. Maintaining differentiation and willingness to pay is the essence of monetization.

6 **Adjust your offer and pricing as customers change behavior.** New business and pricing models mean new types of data. Very dynamic and rich. How do you enrich your pricing decisions with data about customer behaviors, usage patterns, and performance? Within a given pricing model, customers permanently change usage or formulate new requests. This process is constantly evolving and requires many adjustments to your offer over time. These changes must be reflected in your pricing. Are you well equipped to handle these continuous changes to your offer and your current pricing model?

7 **Know when to transition to another pricing model.** Just as your overall business model must evolve when your entire business environment changes, your pricing model must

also evolve when critical milestones are reached. Think ahead about critical pivot points on your roadmap of different pricing models. How do they impact your profit and sales? What will trigger a pivot? How do you transition from one model to another?

8 Build customization into your pricing approach. Across industries, the trend is toward building more flexibility into pricing according to usage, customer-perceived value, and willingness to pay. Are you ready to build more flexibility into the pricing of your digital offers? What roadblocks need to be removed?

Besides the transition in pricing models, is your company ready for pricing model innovation? Where do you stand in the pricing sophistication and maturity level? In 2015, McKinsey & Company proposed several pricing options under the topic of pricing innovation: (1) *ticket to play* consists of gathering information about new pricing models and focusing on what competitors are doing, (2) *pushing the boundaries* focuses on implementing changes in your current pricing approach, and (3) *pioneering new models* expands new pricing and business models into new avenues which potentially can become game changers.[13] The more innovative the option, the more sophistication, risk, and investments are required.

The front end of the data monetization process focused on customer knowledge and understanding differentiation value. The back end of the process is focused on pricing, service agreements, and scaling. What happens at the front end of your Data Monetization Roadmap impacts the back end of your journey. Wrong

---

13   Kevin Chan, Jay Jubas, Berenika Kordes, and Melissa Sueling, "Understanding Your Options: Proven Pricing Strategies and How They Work," McKinsey & Company, March 2015.

decisions, wrong assumptions, or incomplete information early on might lead to bad pricing decisions later. In the digital B2B space, the winners are the ones who do all the homework, without cherry-picking and without cutting corners. Are you ready and willing to make that commitment?

10

Step 7: Execute Your Pricing Strategy through Contracts and Service-Level Agreements

Pay-for-outcomes financing deals can function with outcome clarity that can be measured in terms of improved productivity, increased energy efficiency and reduced costs. In an outcomes contract, it must be possible to clearly report and verify all results.
—*Alliance Prom (infrastructure association), Russia*

PUTTING A FORMAL CONTRACT or service-level agreement in place is much more than a perfunctory extension or an obligatory documentation of what you've accomplished in steps 1 through 6. Having the proper contract or service-level agreement in place is the glue between the outcome of your pilot project in cooperation with customers and the reality of implementing your offer. This is again a critical milestone, no matter how well your collaboration with customers has gone so far.

Framing up a contract or a service-level agreement is an essential step that requires a high level of customer intimacy and trust. It's also a complex process that—like all the other processes we've discussed so far—leaves no room for improvisation or shortcuts. Implementing this phase begins with the four familiar imperatives in figure 10.1.

Customers. The customer "C" means that you both manage and meet customer expectations. The challenge is to give customers "exactly" what they need. When you have an output- or outcome-based contract, the goal is to meet customer expectations consistently and to avoid both under- and overdelivering. Falling short disappoints customers, while exceeding expectations may drive up costs without a corresponding improvement in customer satisfaction or may upset the customer's financial planning. As irrational as it may sound, customers are happy to see better performance but reluctant to pay for it unless they've already made room for the extra expenditure.

Costs. The cost "C" is about cost control. You want to remain in a sweet spot between customer expectations and costs to preserve your margins. Even slight deviations over time can evolve into permanent scope creep, with unexpectedly higher costs and limited upside benefits for you as a supplier. Conversely, aggressive

Customers
Costs
Competition
Change

Figure 10.1. The four imperatives of digital pricing.

cost-cutting is not recommended if it puts your ability to deliver on customer expectations at risk.

Competition. The competition "C" is about benchmarking and monitoring competitors' offers. You need to monitor competition vigilantly and benchmark yourself, *because that's precisely what your customers are doing.* It's in customers' interests to know at all times what their next-best alternative is; therefore, it's in your interest as well. You need that competitive anchor.

Change. The change "C" is about flexibility and adaptability. Any contract or service-level agreement has a set of standards or references whose relevance will erode over time. As circumstances change, how should you adapt, and how should the contract terms evolve? How do you design your first contract with renewal in mind? Many difficulties with complex contracts become apparent only after launch; they're hard to anticipate and plan for. The challenge lies in maintaining the agility and flexibility on both sides rather than sticking stubbornly to performance indicators or terms that were derived from what is now incomplete, incorrect, or outdated information.

Contracts are co-created jointly with customers

Conventional approaches relying on arm's-length contract negotiations do not apply to agreements for the provision of data-enabled services. How do both parties ensure that the contract has both the precision and the flexibility to drive mutual profitability over a period of three to five years? The idea of co-incubation and collaboration does not end once the prototyping and piloting phases are completed. The contract itself must also be designed and executed jointly by both parties. There is too much complexity, and too many contingencies, during a lengthy contract-execution period to have one side unilaterally dictate or control the terms.

The process map for preparing a contract is shown in figure 10.2. Pricing models form the foundation for these contracts, but many outcome-based contracts or service-level agreements do not specify a single price point. Michelin's fleet management solutions for tires may serve as a good illustration. A Michelin customer's fleet may comprise several thousand trucks and trailers with different vehicle types, running situations, and usage patterns. This requires an array of price points that must be defined, mutually agreed upon, and stipulated in a contract. How does Michelin ensure that it isn't signing up for losses? Part of the answer is that the supplier and the customer create a joint contract-execution team who act as the "guardians" for correctly implementing the contract over time. This is why contract design and execution represent an integrated process with joint teams and aligned objectives.

Continuing with the Michelin example, if the customer's truck drivers change their driving behavior, after an agreement is signed, in a way that is not aligned with the contract, one cannot wait until the damage is done. The right KPI needs to be in place to help identify a problem early and trigger a need for intervention, such as driver retraining or new incentives. This example also underlines the critical role of data for the execution of outcome-based contracts. Customers must be transparent with usage data. A customer can't claim that poor execution of the contract is both the sole responsibility and the sole burden of the supplier. The

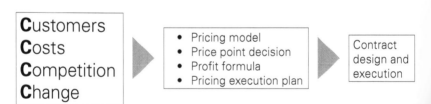

Figure 10.2. Process steps for developing a contract or service-level agreement.

customer and supplier must work closely together and align their resources and activities so that both parties are responsible for achieving the agreed-on KPIs.

In the end, chances are that your analysis of the 4 C's might lead to the definition of a complex pricing strategy including a blend of pricing models. As you recall, we called this a hybrid model. The difficulty then is to translate this complexity into robust service contracts that integrate specific general sales conditions related to digital. GE's Predix pricing model is a good example of such complexity.

(main text continues on page 229)

GE Predix Pricing Model Complexity

GE Digital pricing strategy[1]

- IoT solution includes, most of the time, several components (hardware, software, services . . .).
- This could drive a complicated pricing model.
- GE Digital used a value-based pricing strategy to align its prices with the value they deliver and with "how customers make money."
- These models became the center of its pricing strategy.
- GE Digital also offers an ROI calculator for creating tailored value models and accelerating customer engagement.

Predix Platform pricing

- The Predix Platform is priced competitively with other PaaS providers on like-for-like capabilities with three

---

1   http://www.spmgglobal.com/single-post/2017/02/07/How-GE-Creates-and-Captures-Value-in-the-Industrial-Internet-Era

packages according to customer type: Professional, Premium, and Enterprise.[2]

	Professional (small)	Premium (medium)	Enterprise (large)
Edge	$204,000/year	$936,000/year	$3,768,000/year
	Alternative pricing per device		
Cloud (core)	$132,000/year	$324,000/year	$552,000/year
Cloud (asset/ analytics)	$48,000/year	$240,000/year	$468,000/year
Apps		*Call for quote*	

Applications pricing

- GE has a separate pricing model for each application.[3]

4 types of pricing *(see appendix):*

1 Per usage with a fixed price per unit
2 Per usage with tiered prices
3 Fixed prices with several options
4 Fixed price, only one option

▶ In some case, GE offers two pricing options for the same offer.
▶ For several applications, GE offers a free trial (1-month free trial or free under a fixed usage).

---

2   https://www.ge.com/digital/sites/default/files/Global-Partner
     -Summit-2017-Predix-Pricing-Use-Cases-Justin-LaChance-Jason
     -Seay.pdf
3   https://www.predix.io/catalog/services

Units used depend on the application:

- Per user
- Per managed device
- Per object connected
- Per GB
- Per instance
- Per update
- Per credit (several credits needed for a special transaction)
- Per query per month
- . . .

▶ In some cases, customer has the choice between two units of measure (e.g., per object or per instance)
   All these options are driving an unclear picture in terms of pricing for customers.[4]

Appendix—Example GE Digital applications pricing options

- Fixed price per month + per usage with a fixed price per unit[5]

Feature	Price
Managed subscriptions	$10.00 per subscription per month
Usage events	$0.05 per usage event collected

---

4   https://forum.predix.io/questions/8198/predix-cost-calculator.html
5   https://www.predix.io/services/service.html?id=1231

- Per usage with tiered prices[6]

	Updates	Per update per month
Tier 1	First 10K	$0.000
Tier 2	Next 990K	$0.000249
Tier 3	Next 49M	$0.000219
Tier 4	Next 450M	$0.000199
Tier 5	Next 4.5B	$0.000189
Tier 6	Over 5B	$0.000184

- Fixed prices with several options[7]

Plan	Price per month	API credits allowed per month
Free	$0	2.5K API credits
50K API credits	$500	50K API credits
100K API credits	$1,000	100K API credits
500K API credits	$5,000	500K API credits
1M API credits	$10,000	1M API credits

- Fixed price per month, only one option[8]

Plan	Standard
Price per month	$5
Free trial	30 days

---

6   https://www.predix.io/services/service.html?id=2120
7   https://www.predix.io/services/service.html?id=1624
8   https://www.predix.io/services/service.html?id=1186

(*continued from page 225*)

Redefining pricing excellence

Outcome-based pricing isn't for everyone. Many organizations and many customers lack the resources, expertise, risk tolerance, commitment, or data and analytical skills needed to make these joint efforts work successfully and sustainably over a period of years. Yet outcome-based pricing can often be an attractive avenue for capturing more value in a market.

For decades, the idea of pricing excellence resided in the area represented by the left-hand box in figure 10.3. This is one reason why this kind of thinking—and the dry, arm's-length contract negotiations that accompany it—is so entrenched and so hard to dislodge. Then suppliers began to recognize the potential

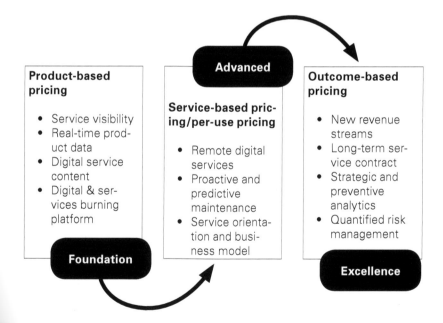

Figure 10.3. How the standard for pricing excellence has evolved.

of capturing more value through services beyond their product core. In recent years, many B2B companies have evolved from *selling products* to *selling value*. Thus, naturally, the emphasis shifted over time from *selling boxes* to *selling asset efficiency*, asset availability, or asset usage. That brings us to the "advanced" area in the middle box. Ultimately, suppliers are tempted to shift to the far right, where a company sells outcomes achieved according to the jobs that customers ultimately want to get done. On the left, parties remain in a logic of transactional pricing. On the right, the contract must govern the entire ongoing relationship between the two parties. A straightforward maintenance contract based on an "if it breaks, we'll fix it" approach is far different from a relationship in which the customer and its supplier jointly manage and monitor performance achievements.

But you can only prepare and execute that kind of contract when you have a deep understanding of all risk factors involved. Data, analytical skills, and agreement on the right KPIs help to mitigate that. The complexity of contracts and the magnitude of risk involved often discourage companies from moving to the right depicted in figure 10.3. In many industries, only a few firms venture into full-fledged outcome-based contracts—for a good reason: a supplier needs the required resources and skills to muster such complex agreements. Not every company, though, needs to move to the far right of figure 10.3. There's a happy life for many suppliers in the "advanced" stage—unleashing profit potential through advanced offers built around asset optimization without assuming responsibility for entire processes or parts thereof.

Types of contracts

The contract that you develop jointly with customers is a function of the type of service relationship you want to establish with them. Figure 10.4 summarizes three types of service contracts.

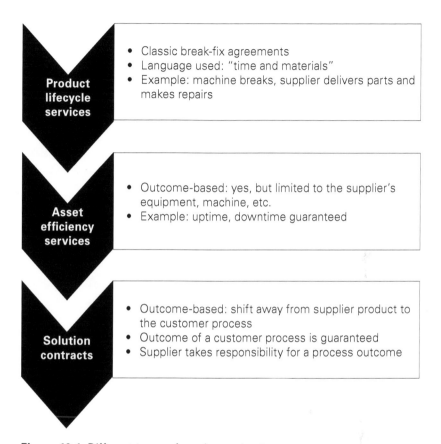

Figure 10.4. Different types of service contracts.

Contracts designed around traditional product life-cycle services focus on traditional break-fix agreements. Suppliers invoice customers on the basis of resources allocated: time spent, spare parts needed, and so forth (e.g., "time and material"). The second type of contract moves from a focus on resources needed to outcomes achieved. These outcomes focus solely on the vendor's product, such as a packaging machine installed or a medical device deployed. Outcome-based contracts in this second category refer to asset efficiency (e.g., uptime guarantee) and typically require data-enabled services, such as remote monitoring, among others. The third type of contract also focuses on outcomes. However, here the scope of performance guarantees made by a vendor encompasses entire customer processes and/or parts thereof. As a consequence, KPIs change dramatically. For example, when signing a solution contract with a car manufacturer, an automotive coating supplier is paid as a function of the number of flawlessly painted vehicles leaving the production line, not according to volume of coatings sold.

(*main text continues on page 237*)

Essentials for Performance-Based Contracts

For performance-based pricing, suppliers must[1]

- define the **performance standard level** that meets customer's requirements (minimum of service acceptable)
- define how the performance will be measured and provide a **framework to monitor the performance** (clearly specified in mutually agreed-upon, definitive, and quantitative terms)

All key performance indicators (KPIs) used in the framework are **different in each contract**.
Several KPIs can be used to measure performance:

- Customer satisfaction
- Work-order completion times
- Workforce productivity

---

1   Facility Engineering Associates, 2012: https://www.feapc.com
    /wp-content/uploads/2012/09/Performance-Based-Contracting.pdf

Example of metrics:

Metric	Std.	Metric	Std.
Facility condition index	<0.05	Stockroom turns/year	2–3
Deferred maintenance backlog	Trend	Annual training hours	<40
On-the-job wrench time	>60%	Maintenance cost/ replacement cost	3–4%
PM/CM ratio	70/30	Return work	<5%
Unscheduled maintenance downtime	<2%	Mean time between failures	Trend
PM schedule compliance	>95%	% failures assessed: root cause	>75%
CM schedule compliance	>90%	Maintenance OT percentage	5–15%
Unscheduled work hours	<10%	% WO covered by estimates	>90%
WO turnaround time	Trend	On-site supervisor time	>65%
Emergency response time	<15 min	Stockroom on-time delivery	>97%
Stockroom service level	>97%	Material/part performance	>98%

In a performance-based contract, both **internal inputs** (quality control [QC]) and **external outputs** (quality assurance [QA]) need to be measured:

- Quality control: measurement of the quality of inputs (training, tools, staff . . .)
- Quality assurance: measurement of the quality of outputs (inspections, data monitoring, customer surveys)

The **quality and transparency of metrics** is important in order to . . .

- monitor the performance and ensure that the contract terms are met
- detect early problems
- prevent fraud and avoid conflicts
- encourage communication and strong partnership

The use of **digital technology** is one of the keys. "Companies need to use this digital technology (wearables, sensors, and IoT applications) to capture, analyze, and then act on the new insight to deliver the agreed-upon outcomes with the highest efficiency, tweaking products and services along the way as required."[2]

Understanding of customer's business and **partnering** are also essential in performance-based pricing: "Trust, respect and cooperation replacing traditional confrontation." In addition, the **governance** structures need to deliver transparency and visibility for both sides.[3] A performance-based contract "can turn into a costly, risky exercise that delivers unpredictable results. Customers don't always get the outcomes they expect." **Sharing risks** need to be considered in such contracts: sharing gains and pains, for example.[4]

Example: Honeywell, Assurance 360

Offer:

- Created in 2013
- Maintains, supports, and optimizes the performance of Honeywell control systems

2   Harvard Business Review: https://hbr.org/2016/09
     /what-to-know-before-you-sign-a-payment-by-results-contract
3   Paul O'Hare, Head of Outsourcing, Kemp Little LLP / NOA Council
     member: http://www.gsa-uk.com/documents/Outcome
     -based%20contracting:%20Past,%20present%20and%20future
4   Juan Crosby, Partner, PwC Legal LLP / NOA Council member:
     http://www.gsa-uk.com/documents/Outcome
     -based%20contracting:%20Past,%20present%20and%20future

- Provides remote monitoring, change management, risk mitigation, technology upgrade, and new installation support and performance-based metrics and reporting

Pricing model (Assurance 360, Optima):

- Pay-per-performance pricing
- Assurance 360 Optima gets users out of the transactional world and focuses on outcomes
- When customers make money, Honeywell makes money

Two service levels:

	ASSURANCE 360 Performa (Assist)	ASSURANCE 360 Optima (Do)
Offer baseline	Predict and Resolve	Predict and Support
Contract type	**Co-sourced** ▶ Honeywell has an advisory role	**Outsourced** ▶ Honeywell both advises and directly handles tasks
Resources	Offer expert help, but no onsite management	Dedicated onsite performance manager responsible for managing all incidents
Change implementation	**Done by the customer** Honeywell only recommends changes and practices	**Done by Honeywell**
Pricing	**Standard method** • Honeywell oversight of outcomes • Honeywell not compensated based on the results	**Pay-for-performance** • Honeywell ownership of outcomes • Outcomes define revenue paid • Creation of performance metrics and scorecards (compensation is determined on these scorecard results)

Metrics:

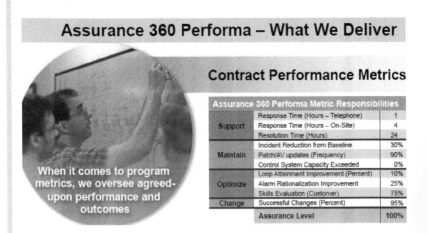

Extracted from https://www.honeywellprocess.com/library/news-and
-events/presentations/Honeywell-Assurance-360.pdf on 06/05/2018

(*continued from page 232*)

Recommendations and caveats for developing a contract

In our experience, developing a contract is complex and time-consuming even in the best of cases. To avoid making the process even more intricate, we've developed several recommendations and offer you a few caveats.

- **Get your legal team involved early.** Obviously a contract or service agreement is a legal document. And of course, legal teams in B2B companies have the reputation implied by the nickname "Mr. and Ms. No," because they seem to reflexively reject new ideas and give lengthy answers for why something can't or shouldn't be done. They can be a complete buzzkill for an enthusiastic development team. But we can't underestimate their impact on contract negotiations, because of their ability to anticipate and prevent surprises and to supply clarity around terms, definitions, rights, and so forth.

  No one expects your predictions of the future, as manifested in the contract and in your KPIs, to be perfect. Adjustments will be necessary. But neither you nor the customer should ever be blindsided by an event or contingency that could undermine your relationship. So your legal team should be involved early in the MVP development process and the contract drafting. They can advise on whether you've defined terms clearly and unambiguously and whether you've overlooked an important detail or contingency.
- **Conduct thorough risk analyses.** These analyses, which we also described in chapter 9, must cover operational, financial, and security risks. This applies to both usage- and outcome-based pricing models. This is another area where

transparency, data sharing, and customer intimacy play decisive roles. You can't assess risks properly unless both parties show all their cards.

- **Allocate enough time.** Rushing this process is a risk factor in itself. You risk errors of omission if you prioritize a fast agreement over a sound one. This is especially true for outcome-based pricing models. Don't underestimate the time it takes to prepare and reach agreement with the customer.

- **Define outcomes precisely.** This is a major reason why your legal team needs to be involved early, why risk analysis is critical, and why the contracting process takes time. Let's say for the sake of simplicity that you agree with a customer to lower their energy costs by 10 percent. What do energy costs comprise? How many of these drivers are within your (or the customer's) influence? If you're aiming for this outcome for building management in major cities, what happens if those regions experience a record-cold winter and the oil prices spike because of unrest and currency fluctuations? What happens if tenants change behavior? You need to model the past, define all your terms, and assess and model contingencies.

- **Educate customers.** Be prepared to educate some customers on performance- and outcome-based contracts as well as the measurement, modeling, and commitments involved. It's in your interest to make sure the customer is a smart, informed, eye-level partner. Again, this kind of relationship is not for every customer. Customers must be prepared and willing to enter into such a far-reaching agreement. If some customers or segments lack digital maturity, you need to decide whether it's worth your while to "train them up" or whether to prioritize customers whose digital maturity and readiness make them better partners in the short term.

- **Define and codify penalties.** Be ready to discuss penalties for noncompliance, but insist also on including rewards when, for example, the customer implements process improvements but incurs short-term costs to do so.
- **Review KPIs.** This is related to the point above about defining an outcome. You need a thorough definition, understanding, and review of KPIs, performance calculations, and sources of data. You also need to distinguish between internal inputs (e.g., quality control, value creation) and external outputs (quality assurance, value delivery). Likewise, you need to distinguish between controllable and uncontrollable variables. Internal quality control means measuring the quality of your inputs (tools, staff, efficiency, waste, etc.), and external quality assurance includes validation through inspections, data monitoring, customer surveys, and so forth. You need to monitor every partner's performance, ensure that contract terms are met, detect problems (fraud, conflicts, flawed assumptions) early, encourage open communication, and continuously improve all along contract execution.
- **Understand roles of other partners.** Think back to the value constellation. The creation of value in data-enabled services often involves the contributions of multiple suppliers and the active participation of your customers' customers. This adds an additional layer of complexity to the contract-execution process.

Data is the lifeblood of contract implementation and partnership success. You must ensure that you have access to data, that data continues to flow throughout all stages of contract execution, that you can properly analyze data, and that you can then take corrective actions—positive or negative—based on what the data reveal. Consider General Electric's example of "outcome as a service," a program actively promoted by GE's Power division, which serves utilities, independent power producers, and power distributors. The concept is an example of GE's infrastructure-as-a-service model. GE knows customers' infrastructure so well, and has access to the data, that it's in a position to guarantee a certain level of performance and to make payment contingent on meeting that performance level.

We mention that kind of guarantee not as a recommendation but rather as an illustration. Think about the data that GE would need in order to offer that guarantee with some level of confidence that it will meet the target. Then think of the data you would need to make the same kind of promise (regardless of whether you offer it). The more customer intimacy you have, the better you can craft and design such contracts, knowing that you'll be able to deliver and can reassure customers of that. Other industrial companies in the energy and utility sector have also adopted risk-sharing agreements: for example ABB, SKF, and Wärtsilä.

Data rights: Be sure you can really get and use what you need

Data has many uses that add value beyond your one-to-one relationship with a customer. One of these is the power of benchmarking from accumulated time series of rich data. Most if not all customers want to know where they stand relative to comparable companies, but you can't help them understand that unless enough customers have pooled their data in anonymized form for you to analyze. You can't just assume that you have the rights to use any data for any purpose unless that purpose is explicitly spelled out in the contract. Think back to chapter 8, on data and trust. Contractual agreements must clearly stipulate how data may be accessed and used. We list some of the relevant issues in figure 10.5.

The degree of customer intimacy we've discussed and the steps described in this book will expose you to mind-boggling possibilities in terms of what data is available, what you could theoretically use it to do, and how much value those applications and insights contain. At the same time, customers will be cautious about whom to trust and what to share. To ensure that both parties agree on what data is exchanged and how it will be used, you must include a section on data rights in any contract.

Contracts, like everything else in this book, are about building mutual trust. The more a company moves into digitally driven offers and outcome-based contracts, the more it must develop new contract-writing competencies and skills in this domain. Having the right people with the right skills thus becomes a factor critical to success. Rather than viewing contracts and service-level

---

Data rights in your contracts or SLAs

- Right to collect the data
- Right to connect the data
- Right to use and benchmark the data
- Right to transfer or sell the data

Data is the new gold

- Inform users about the data sources
- Transparency with data rights creates trust
- Consider cost of data in future models
- Include data rights and privacy clauses in contracts
- Make data security one of your priorities

Figure 10.5. Contractual agreements must stipulate how you can access and use data.

agreements for digital offers as a nuisance or necessary evil, we suggest that you see this step as a critical milestone in turning your concepts and prototypes into reality. Developing unique competencies in this domain may allow you to create a competitive advantage and lay the foundations for monetizing data more profitably than your competitors.

11

Step 8: Transfer and Scale the Opportunity into the Core Business

The plural of anecdote *is not* data.

—*Ben Goldacre*

WE ALL KNOW PETER Drucker's famous expression that "culture eats strategy for breakfast." The reality is that culture could also eat and digest new business models, innovative digital service concepts, and transformative change initiatives. Anyone can have good intentions and consider new subscription-based, pay-per-use, and outcome-based pricing models. But far fewer people prepare well and focus on change management and execution in the digital space. When digital journeys began in earnest years ago, companies acquired more data-driven organizations. These moves made sense, but many of the acquiring companies did not prepare enough to adequately integrate these firms.

Without a proper effort in this domain, great ideas get destroyed, smothered by existing process routines, conflicting priorities, and a lack of training, just to name a few root causes.

Imagine that you have 150 experienced salespeople who have sold products, equipment, and components for many years. Now you suddenly ask them to sell a digital service offering and discuss with customers software licenses, a subscription to a new app, or access to a digital platform. Overnight you've effectively changed the job descriptions for dozens if not hundreds of people—customer service reps, technical support reps, application engineers, salespersons—"simply" because you transitioned to a go-to-market model. You can't simply tell your salespeople, "We deployed a new outcome-based pricing model. Go sell it!"

Talk about a huge complication for an established team! And this is not the only team who will be disrupted. Consider the finance team, who now must integrate all revenue recognition, invoicing, and taxation issues. During our expert interview for this book, a senior finance executive shared his own experience with us. It took his team nine months to integrate a new software pricing model into his company's legacy ERP system. The impact was brutal on the ability of the salesforce to sell the licenses. The major issue was calculating a bill of material for a license versus a traditional product. This is the type of small detail that will impact your organization's ability to launch and scale data-driven offers.

In all seriousness, though, what's the right time to announce and implement such major changes? After all, you've worked very hard, and we assume that you've successfully executed the first seven steps of the Data Monetization Roadmap. But your process isn't done after you've tested the prototype, conducted customer pilots, and maybe already sold your first digital offers to customers. So what happens next? Who will answer fundamental questions, such as these:

- Who will sell our solution?
- How will they sell it, and to whom?
- What happens with existing distribution partners?
- How do we incentivize them?
- How do we train them?

The more innovative your pricing models, the more you need to answer those questions thoroughly, diligently, and—above all—early. This is why we added a final step to the Data Monetization Roadmap to address the transfer of the offers you'll commercialize into your core business. It's not the role of the incubator or the digital teams to ramp up and scale these opportunities. They lack the needed infrastructure, incentives, and sales teams. Transferring these offers back to the core business is essential.

You can't wait until the last minute to worry about the transfer plan. You need to create some kind of a transfer package and a scale plan, developed and implemented by a cross-functional team. Figure 11.1 lays out the whole process from ideation to transfer.

Transferring and scaling your offer is a fundamental step in the innovation process, not an afterthought or a denouement. A great idea is not great unless you can make this transfer. And nothing that's getting transferred should be news to the sales team or to any other team that needs to scale the data-based offer from within the core business.

We recommend that you include a formal gate for transfer in your Data Monetization Roadmap, meaning that no formal transfer occurs without the approval of a committee or a gate team. The incubator is responsible for planning and making the transfer. That means laying the groundwork not only on their side of the gate but also on the other side at the core business. The team at the incubator cannot merely force the digital offer through the gate

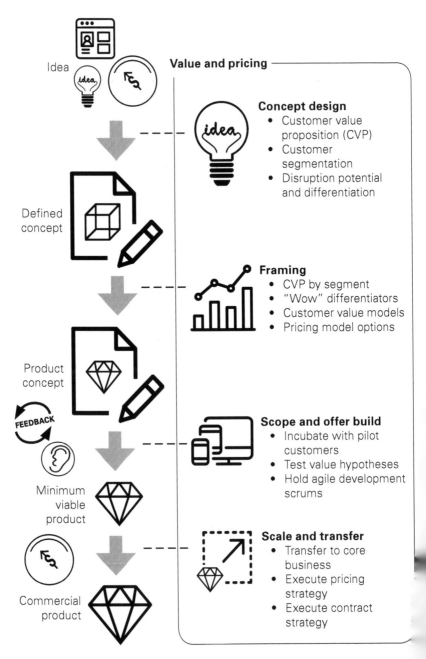

Figure 11.1. Scale and transfer is a fundamental step in the innovation process.

or "throw it over the wall," to use the classic R&D cliché. There has to be a way in place for the core business to absorb the new digital offer to be commercialized. You can serve your offer to the core business on a silver platter, but to apprehend and digest what's on that platter, the core business needs utensils, manners, and appetite. In other words, they need the tools, the processes and guidelines, the full context, and the motivation to make the new digitally driven offer a success on a much larger scale.

Turning your new digital initiative into a commercially viable offering requires a practical approach and awareness of potential constraints in the core business. Let's assume that your MVP exits the incubator and is ready to be scaled in the spring of the new fiscal/calendar year. The budgeting cycle, however, begins in the summer and ends in the fall of the current fiscal year. If you haven't budgeted for training, marketing plans, and other resources well in advance, you can't finance your scaling, and your offer will sit in limbo until the next cycle. If scaling requires ten additional salespeople, you won't have them and won't get them. These are two simple examples to underscore our point: you need to begin planning the transfer process very early and ensure that the core business is fully ready to begin when the new digital offer arrives. Your core business teams may be good, but no one can work overnight magic. You need to put those teams in the best advance position to succeed.

Another way to look at this is illustrated in figure 11.2. In your incubator or innovation hub, you can only do a limited number of customer pilots, during which you'll undergo a process of deep learning. But you can't go straight from customer pilots to customer prospecting—straight from the top box to the bottom box—without some kind of processing and planning. The learnings from the co-incubation and the pilots must be generalized, projected, and transitioned into tools, reference case studies, segment-specific value propositions, and pricing guidelines that the sales teams can employ under the commercial scaling plan.

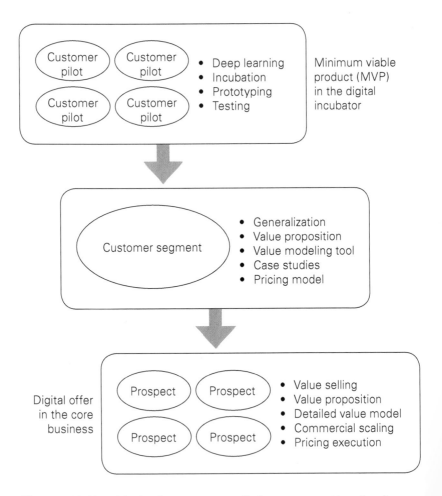

Figure 11.2. Transitioning from customer piloting to prospecting: An often-neglected step.

This is the bridge step in the middle of figure 11.2, a step that's incomplete or even neglected in many companies. This work in this intermediate phase could involve the creation of value-model calculators, an IoT calculator, or the design of a turnkey solution depending on the size, maturity, and needs of the segments. It's not a step back or a detour. Rather, it's a necessary interpretation codification, and translation of what you've learned. Short-circuiting the sequence in figure 11.2, either by jumping to the intermediate phase too early or by jumping directly to the final phase, puts the success of your data monetization initiative at risk. Without a proper transition, the core business won't be able to help customers understand it, appreciate it, and ultimately buy it.

(main text continues on page 251)

Making the Most from Pricing Offers and Negotiating with Customers: Is Your Salesforce On Board for Selling Digital Services?

You need to transfer your digital prototype from the incubator to your core business so that the new offer will gain commercial traction. This requires tackling many practical questions, such as finalizing marketing collateral, setting prices, and so forth. But most of all, during this stage, you need to secure buy-in from your commercial teams regarding the key marketing and sales issues. Be aware that your salesforce can make or break the success of your offer at this critical stage.

From working with firms on monetizing data, we have experienced firsthand one of the most nagging problems: the temptation to invoice a new digital service way below value created or—even worse—giving away digital services for free. Over the past years, Ulaga & Associés, a management consulting firm in France, has worked with multiple customers on turning around services, including digital offers, from "free to fee" (F2F), in other words, transforming profit drains into profit gains.

Don't get us wrong. Suppliers may have good reasons for offering a digital service for free, with a deliberate strategy in mind. However, digital services are often given away for free, especially in the early commercialization stage, because of the lack of a deliberate pricing strategy, including blind spots about competitors' actions, fear, inertia, or resistance to change—more often than not from within the sales organization.

Beyond forgone revenue and profit opportunities, giving digital services away unthinkingly sends the wrong signals to customers, employees, and partners in your value constellation. But most of all: once you've educated everyone that "free" is the norm, it's very hard to turn back the wheel.

To address this challenge, Ulaga & Associés has developed a three-step roadmap for turning free digital services into revenue generators. Managers must first take stock of the revenue and profit opportunities and generate internal awareness of the magnitude of the potential at stake. They then must build a company-specific action plan for adequately pricing new offers or turning around free digital services. To this end, companies can use a five-step decision framework separating most attractive from least attractive revenue opportunities. Finally, executives need to drive pricing transitions strategically and address resistance to change, whether from within (salespeople, frontline technicians) or outside (customers, competitors, partners). Typically met arguments range all the way from "charging for this new digital offer will turn them against us," and "there's nothing we can do; competition doesn't invoice for benchmarking data," to "we have no idea what remote monitoring is worth to customers; let's bundle it into an all-inclusive price to get more equipment sales done."

Interestingly, internal resistance is often stronger than customers' lack of willingness to pay for new digital offers. As one executive stated, "When customers see the value we provide, they are happy to pay. Our biggest challenges are not on our customers' side; it's our own people we have to convince."

Asking customers to pay for digital services might place salespersons in an uncomfortable position. Yet, the best strategy is to move from pricing anxiety to pricing confidence

Tough negotiations create stress for salespeople, who must cope with customers' negative reactions, face uncertainty, and deal with potential rejection. Systematic training, including roleplaying, professional feedback, sharing of best practices, and celebrating early successes can greatly enhance salespersons' pricing confidence, together with corporate support in the form of value documentation tools and reference customer cases. Nonetheless, not all salespeople will be able or willing to embark on the journey. To succeed, you must revisit how you hire, train, incentivize, and lead your salesforce to ensure digital services growth.

For additional information on F2F pricing and sales transformation for digital services, read the article in *Sloan Management Review*, "Bill It, Kill It, or Keep It?" by Wolfgang Ulaga and Stefan Michel.

(continued from page 249)

The commercial scaling plan in more detail

We've seen that one key success factor is to begin early with the planning for the transfer to the core business and to plan for commercial scaling. Likewise, we've said that the commercial scaling plan requires a second critical element: an intermediate step where you combine concepts and prototypes with your deep customer learnings to create the value documentation, reference cases, and sales tools that will hook your prospects. But how do you make that work? Figure 11.3 highlights some of the key steps and tasks in developing these plans. You need to establish your RACI matrix (Responsible-Accountable-Consulted-Informed) by identifying the people and teams that will design and lead the transition, sell your new offering, monitor and manage the financials, and track the speed and intensity of the scaling.

The final point in figure 11.3 is particularly important. During the incubation period, your teams have worked closely with

Prepare early for commercial reentry in the core business and for scaling

- Digital opportunity accountability
- Commercial development plan (who will sell?)
- Responsibility for the innovation roadmap
- Execution of pricing strategies and guidelines
- Business model financials execution
- Scaling plan execution and speed
- Management of critical partnerships (software, data providers, content, etc.)

Figure 11.3. Tasks and steps for preparing your commercial plans.

external partners on an aggressive path to develop the new data-enabled offering. When the commercial scaling begins, these partnerships will be managed by people from the core business, who may have ideologies, viewpoints, priorities, skills, and behaviors that are different from those of the teams in your incubator. You must therefore prepare these key partners for the transition to prevent hiccups or conflicts after the transfer.

The transfer package must include several aspects that flesh out the pricing models and anchor them in the realities of the core business and the customers it serves. To keep things simple, we keep the basic "customer-cost-competition-change" model in mind, which we elaborated early in chapter 10. The pricing "deliverables" include a dollarized value model and a pricing model by customer segment. You also need an overarching pricing strategy by segment, as well as pricing guidelines and decision-making processes. This list only reinforces what we illustrated in figure 11.2, namely that the shift from piloting to prospecting and scaling requires a dedicated transitioning phase.

Some of the tools that support these deliverables are an estimated cost model and a bill of material, as well as information or competitive price points. Both are subject to variation and even volatility, which means they require constant monitoring. The costs may be harder than usual to identify as your business model switches significantly from selling components, products, or systems to focusing on data-enabled services and customer solutions. What are the costs, what is the new bill of material, and how easily and quickly can you integrate this new critical information in your SAP, Oracle, or whatever ERP system is in place? This isn't a trivial task. As in any other critical milestone on our Data Monetization Roadmap, these are not occasions for improvisation, nor are there magic wands at your disposal.

Two additional points are the pricing execution plan and the pricing accountability plan. The worst outcome of all is that the salespeople attempt to circumvent the new pricing models: "Yeah, subscription-based pricing sounds good, but my customers are used to having our services thrown in for free to help close the deal. Why change?" A critical means to ensure that that doesn't happen is to launch appropriate incentive plans for digital pricing objectives. If your best salespeople have earned their money for years selling hardware to key accounts, how can you integrate incentives for data-enabled services into existing plans in a way that preserves or even increases their motivation?

Your sales reps may experience some awkward moments as they explain the new pricing models and services to customers. What they sell may have the same name, belong to the same category, and be software based, but the customers might balk when they hear that the service has value and that they will now need to pay for it. What's your contingency plan if your sales teams cannot properly sell data-enabled services under the appropriate pricing plans, or if customers resist even their best efforts to switch the basis of the business? Such contingency plans are rarely discussed, but they deserve attention. For a detailed discussion of how to avoid unnecessarily giving new digital service offerings away for free, we refer you to Wolfgang's 2018 *Sloan Management Review* article "Bill It, Kill It, or Keep It?"

You need pricing experts. Plural.

Figure 11.4 shows some of the highly specialized roles that you must fill in order to transfer and scale a digital offer. The challenge of filling those roles with people with the right skill sets and ambition is even greater in companies that lack analogous pricing roles or functions. If those people don't exist today in the core business, how will you accomplish the necessary pricing tasks, whether it's before or during or after the transfer? Who's asking the tough questions and doing the pricing work? Who's in charge

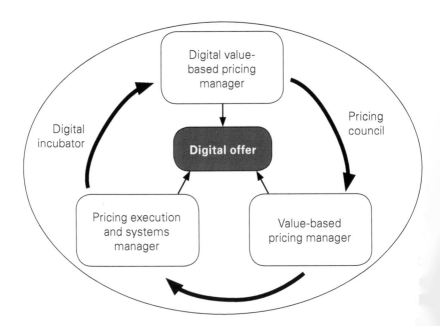

Figure 11.4. The managerial roles for digital or data-enabled offers.

of monetization and dollarization? If you do have a pricing team, why aren't they involved? Such companies would have to bring in consultants or other outside experts to undertake those roles until a permanent set of managers is installed. This isn't a magic wand or "just add water" problem. Bringing on outside people can be expensive, but it's still cheaper than failure.

Figure 11.4 also shows that the work is not complete just because the digital offer is ready to leave the incubator. There needs to be a bridge between the incubator and a pricing committee or pricing council, which hopefully exists already. Pricing expert(s) must be involved for the data monetization effort to succeed. You can't succeed without a pricing champion involved.

To master your data monetization initiative, you need to cover three critical pricing functions. You need someone to manage pricing in the data-enabled world, someone to manage pricing in your core business, and people from systems and execution to integrate the two. Without all three functions and roles in place, the risk of outright failure, or the risk that your organization regresses into a cost-plus habit, is much higher.

You should also have someone who's focused on systems and execution, such as a manager who works with IT on rebates, discounts, and optimization. Some large B2B tech companies even have individual managers for each of these areas. All these managers need to interact and communicate so that new data-enabled services reach the market as if coming from one company and not from a disjointed or divided organization.

We highlight this issue here because we learned in our work with B2B companies that the existing pricing teams in the core business are rarely involved in the work of a firm's digital incubator. This is a loss and a shame on many fronts. First, mission-critical pricing expertise fails to flow into the planning and decision-making processes while the digital offering is still in incubation. Second, the incubator risks producing something that's a poor fit with t: core business, making the transfer harder to plan and execu Third, the pricing manager touches many other functions—fro sales to marketing to IT—and is thus an important contributor the incubation and development process and to the commerc scaling plan, not just the narrower pricing-related issues.

You shouldn't underestimate the importance of integrati: IT into the transfer planning, beginning early in the incubati phase. Some B2B managers we worked with insist that the d logue with IT should be established early on, because of the pot tial lead times required and the assessment of data quality a needs. Your company may find it hard to establish recurring b ing cycles to collect customer payments for data-enabled servic under a subscription model. Others may have difficulties securi: the financing for installment payments. Some of the pricing m els we discussed require entirely different forms of accounting. you can't provide adequate support in the form of an efficient a effective IT/ERP infrastructure that's ready to go when you ma the transfer, you're in trouble. The main bottleneck is usually tir not resources, so make sure you inform IT early, adjust supp infrastructures, and fill those critical managerial roles.

This marks the final step in the Data Monetization Roadm You might think that eight steps for a roadmap are a lot giv the speed of digital business growth and the need to devel data-driven offers very quickly. Time pressures are a real But the need to focus on the critical steps of developing robt data-enabled offers is not incompatible with speed. We've m tioned several times that there needs to be a clear commitment resources, to robust preparation, and to not taking shortcuts using the roadmap. In the next chapter, we discuss organizatior challenges that typically arise as you make the transfer and beg the commercial scaling.

12

Don't Underestimate Organizational Considerations

Digital transformation is all about learning. Not only must you learn to master new technologies, but you have to learn about new business models, new pricing models, new ecosystems, new customer and employee experience... A company cannot transform without a deep learning agenda!
—*Pierre Schaeffer, SVP & CMO, Thales Group*

MANY PEOPLE SEEK THE adrenaline rush of the exhilarating world of data-enabled digital services. They read exciting reports from top consulting firms and get very energized after attending the numerous presentations at conferences or online. But who will do the dirty work that doesn't involve buzzwords and flashy presentations? Everyone wants to work in digital and deal with data, but no one wants to sign up for the hard work and embark on the journey full of obstacles to overcome.

But that sums up the challenges that an organization faces when it seeks to merge the innovativeness of a digital incubator with the strengths of the core business to make data-enabled B2B offers an enduring success. This is why B2B companies working on monetizing data also must conduct a digital transformation at their core.

Merging the strengths of these markedly different business styles begins with recognizing the potential barriers. To succeed, firms must deploy a comprehensive digital learning agenda focused on changing and aligning the mindsets in both the digital and the core businesses. In the following pages, we discuss ten main challenges we've identified based on interviewing executives about their experience and grounded in our own experience of working with companies in this space. When "digital ideas meet traditional business," managers must be mindful of the following issues.

1 **Competing agendas.** Imagine that several divisions are competing to establish a company's first predictive maintenance platform. That intense internal competition may sound healthy at first. But these parallel efforts will dilute the attention and resources of the organization. Furthermore, the teams will not communicate with each other in the midst of competition. The worst-kept secret in such organizations is that competition will eventually force a day of reckoning. You need to make informed decisions based on your organization's best capabilities, best time to market, and best customer pilots rather than listen to divisions claiming *ownership* and trying to be the first to bask in the limelight. Such competition create

unnecessary complexity and wastes resources better used elsewhere. The irony is that a holistic and focused approach—not intracompany competition—gives the whole organization its best chance to win.

2 **A 99 percent focus on design, but just a 1 percent focus on execution.** Leaders in data-enabled businesses often make visually rich presentations with "boil the ocean" concepts. But most of these concepts are impossible to execute within a traditional industrial culture. We've got nothing against vision, but well-polished conceptual presentations and bold intentions raise questions no one wants to answer: How can we get all that stuff done when we can't even get the basics right in the core business? Who's focusing on execution? The wannabe digital organization spends 99 percent of its time focusing on design at the expense of laying out a bridge between concepts and reality, between vision and actual earnings. We recommend that industrial companies skip the boil-the-ocean concepts and remain grounded, especially if the company's organizational culture is still deeply entrenched in a manufacturing-oriented DNA.

3 **The clash of two worlds.** The cleavage between traditional and digital cultures can be devastating when middle and top management do not understand the need for speed and disruption when faced with changing customer needs. Ask yourself this question: are data-enabled services a separate business, or just different offerings within the same business, albeit with different value needs and customer propositions? We argue that they're the latter. Your digital offers should permeate your entire portfolio of market offerings; they should be embedded in your product-, systems-, services-, and customer solution-offering strategy. Digital teams need to stop getting caught up in the cycle of excitement and pretending they know more than

anyone else in the organization. They need to be mindful and to begin to focus on execution and quick wins, on ROI and filtering their MVPs. They also need to be aware of their lack of customer and application experience when communicating with experienced managers in the core business. At the same time, your managers in the core business, trained to focus on results, need to begin understanding what digital teams are doing and why their work is vital to the company's future.

4 **Success is the enemy of change.** When the core business is profitable and growing, it's hard to convince the core teams to help with the hard work on these digital offers. They'll argue that the customers are happy: Why should we rock the boat with these unproven, uncertain propositions that haven't earned a dime? Why should we get customers excited about something that could potentially disrupt an existing, profitable product? We agree that it's hard to put a universally positive spin on a word like *cannibalization*. But this is where the first steps of the Data Monetization Roadmap come into play. Map your value constellation. Conduct your segmentation to identify and group the customers who are ahead of the rest, so that you can target them before they abandon you for someone else's more attractive digital offer. These customers are not necessarily the ones you've been the most successful with. There's always a right answer to the question of whom you should target and whom you should partner with.

5 **Focus, focus, focus.** Investing too little can choke off opportunities. Investing too much can also be detrimental because it can smother strong opportunities under the weight of far too many weaklings. Your digital incubator or digital factory needs to screen for interesting, attractive, and profitable opportunities. The fast and efficient culling of weak projects, however, is difficult in a corporate culture lacking a sense

of confrontation or negative feedback. Yet you must do it! The worst situation is to have 100 percent of the MVPs that enter the digital framing pipeline emerge with a commercial offer. A more acceptable ratio would 1:5 or 1:10 for offers transferred back to the core for commercialization. This level of honesty must also apply to companies that have weak customer intimacy and an unspectacular history of innovation. If you don't spend enough time with customers or you lack a culture of innovation, your data monetization efforts will probably yield a bunch of me-too offers with little or no differentiation and little chance of success, regardless of their value in absolute terms. These companies should first take a step back and build a more customer-centric organization that truly benefits all customer-driven growth efforts, not just digital initiatives.

6 **Speed and agility.** What might be acceptable in the traditional world may not even be feasible in the digital world. Let's be clear: you can't afford slow decision making, and you need to recalibrate your tolerance and perspective on risk management. Do you have teams working to bridge the gaps between core business units and the digital incubators? You need to recognize that one side needs to accelerate its thinking and processes while the other may need to slow down. The same applies to risk management. The time and the need to check all the boxes at the usual pace of the core business may result in a watered-down offer that doesn't meet customer requirements and is delivered to the market too late. This is unacceptable in the digital world.

7 **Deep versus flat hierarchies.** When managers from the core business shift over to work in the digital incubator, two things inevitably happen. First, they lose their navigational marks. Second, they are subject to more accountability and responsibility, because the layers above and below them are

thinner, to the extent that they exist. This is why they struggle at first to make entrepreneurial decisions. Without intervention and education, they can act as a brake rather than as a valuable resource. We recommend meeting this problem head-on. You need to get the managers from the core business comfortable with their new roles. People can rise to the occasion and thrive in the digital environment, and you need a system in place to find these managers and help them strive.

8 **You still need a process.** Process is the glue connecting design and execution. Not everything can be white space. You need some type of foundational, structuring process. Teams need guidance and process tools to manage the development of their digital innovations. This is especially true once the MVP is transferred back into the core business, where nothing gets done outside the process. You need common templates, tools, and software. If you allow every team to use its own models and procedures, there's no way for you to make the necessary side-by-side comparisons when you decide which prototype deserves more resources than the others or has earned the opportunity for commercialization and scaling, and which prototypes should be abandoned. The side-by-side comparison also helps teams defend such decisions.

9 **Accountability.** Moving to data-enabled services can only be sustainable when you achieve short-term results that demonstrate your projects' potential to the internal investors. This means that your digital leadership teams have to be accountable for their decisions, resource allocation, and actions. The outcome of the project-screening process cannot be fuzzy, unmeasurable, and unaccountable. The worst situation is when a team lets an idea proceed because no one objected. You solve this problem by not allowing abstentions. Your team ultimately need to make and defend clear yes/no decisions.

10 Knowledge. Digital teams will not magically acquire technical and go-to-market knowledge. They need training that they can apply to practical tasks. You need both a training agenda and a training budget as part of the digital program, in the incubators and in the core business. Your efforts in data-enabled services are creating powerful pipelines to money. Lots of good intentions and promises are not outcomes; nor are digital offers themselves outcomes. The only outcomes that matter are those that generate revenues and profitability and thereby achieve the company's commercial and financial goals. Beyond training on tools and techniques, you need training around the metrics you'll use to decide what's successful, and around the emphasis on accountability and other factors required to develop and scale successful data-enabled services.

Managing digital offers in the core business

Success depends on your ability to merge the strengths of the digital incubator with the strengths of the core business. This puts the teamwork aspects we refer to in figure 12.1 at the forefront.

Managing digital offers in the core business

- Cross-functional work (including sales)
- Strong team alignment
- Organization in account team
- Rapid prototyping for new customers
- Modeling of customer-specific estimated value
- Speed of execution to scale the platform
- Agile process development and management
- Fidelity to agreed business model

Figure 12.1. Teamwork comes to the forefront.

The digital teams and the core business need to understand each other's daily work and tasks. The multifunctional nature of the digital-offer development process also means that you need different account teams to serve your customers, facilitate rapid prototyping, and improve your execution speed. Finally, these unified teams serve as a powerful cross-check to ensure that both the digital and the core sides keep their focus on implementing all building blocks of the agreed-upon business model.

When people don't want to play along with these new team arrangements and alignments, such resistance is usually a clear symptom of cultural misalignment. Here are three typical examples we have seen repeatedly when working with companies on monetizing data:

- **"We know the customers better."** The core business claims that customers don't see any value in data, or that they expect data and the accompanying offers to be free. They may also say that the customers can do anything data-related better on their own. The answer to such arguments is not to flip each of those claims around in a black-and-white way. The challenge is to find out what the customer really expects, who else they're talking to, and what their capabilities are. Counter-arguing based on true customer insights represents a much more powerful approach.
- **"Not invented here."** In a company well prepared for its entry into data-enabled services, no one should ever be able to make this claim. It should be clear and transparent who from the core business was involved in MVP development, and why. Likewise, it should be clear and transparent—through dedicated communication—what kinds of offers are on the way. Participation is often perception-driven. Merely takin

someone's opinion seriously is sometimes enough to give someone a sense of ownership or a stake in the outcome.

- **"Digital is a fad."** Dinosaurs abound. And they want to survive. So they'll claim that data is a commodity with no value, or that digital will fizzle or bomb like Y2K or other fads. You can't allow the dinosaurs to rule with their "smoke and mirrors" argument. The surest path to their own extinction is to ignore digital and data-enabled services rather than embrace them.

One reliable way to measure whether you've correctly addressed such resistance to change is to listen and observe. Do you still hear the objections explicitly or implicitly? Do the actions of the core team and the digital team match their words? The best way to overcome such resistance to embarking on your digital growth journey is education, which we discuss next.

Use education to evolve your corporate DNA

You can't implement your data monetization initiative without a strong learning agenda. And it's not just training. You need a full learning agenda, properly funded and implemented early. Figure 12.2 shows the steps to meeting the digital learning imperative in a dedicated, forceful way that truly facilitates the transformation of your corporate DNA.

Creating a learning agenda is a huge endeavor. It cannot be an after-the-fact effort once you've begun transferring solutions back to the core business. The planning and execution of this learning agenda should even predate the start of the co-incubation phase with customers. Learning needs to be cross-functional and should emphasize experience, immersion, and hands-on approaches.

Monetizing data: the digital learning imperative

- Establish a deep and wide learning **agenda**
- **Fund** digital long-term learning programs
- Promote **cross-functional** learning
- Embrace **adult** and **experiential** learning
- **Rotate** team through digital learning programs
- Focus on transforming **mindset**
- Focus on digital **tools** with fast and easy access

Figure 12.2. Steps to mutating your own corporate DNA.

Remember that you have teams coming from business units with different levels of knowledge and maturity in all relevant areas.

Upskilling human resources. We split the focus of the learning agenda into two broad areas: upskilling and reskilling. Upskilling digital teams means raising them to a common and high technological standard. Everyone needs a shared working knowledge of key issues relevant to your digital initiatives, such as AI, augmented reality, connectivity of devices, and cybersecurity, regardless of their respective roles. For the most part, companies do a good job disseminating core knowledge in these domains. Many companies have internal subject-matter experts in these areas, as well as managers and executives who can work with these experts on such topics. What is often neglected in upskilling, though, is the right side of the top box in figure 12.3. Who will ensure that decision makers and designers all share a foundational understanding of business model innovation, value constellation analysis, customer insights, and value-based pricing?

Reskilling human resources. Reskilling business teams is all about mindset and culture. People hear terms such as *growth mindset, speed and agility,* and *customer intimacy,* but they nee

Upskilling digital teams

Educate teams in new digital technologies and go-to-market concepts

- Artificial intelligence
- Big data
- Connectivity
- Cybersecurity

- Business modeling
- System thinking
- Customer insights
- Value-based pricing

Reskilling business teams

Transform mindset to embrace a digital culture

1 Execute with speed and agility
2 Embrace a growth mindset
3 Collaborate and communicate
4 Focus on customer intimacy
5 Manage partnerships and fight NIH

Figure 12.3. Digital learning agenda for upskilling and reskilling teams.

to know in hands-on, practical terms what they mean for the company, what they mean for themselves, and how to apply them each day. Part of this transition can even involve a move away from paper and PowerPoint to e-learning tools that help people appreciate the power of digital transformation firsthand. In most cases you won't have the time or skill to design a proprietary e-platform, so we recommend that you look outside for the simplest, best solution for your teams.

What's the proper data monetization mindset? We show that in figure 12.4, where each point begins with the word *think*. After all, we want people to begin thinking differently, positively, and practically about how new data-enabled offers can help customers derive more value from your expertise and digital offerings.

The data monetization mindset

- Think **function**, not product
- Think **value**, not cost
- Think **value** constellation, not customers
- Think **differentiation**, not you in your silo
- Think **possibility**, not constraints
- Think **opportunity**, not risks
- Think **relationship**, not transactions
- Think **recurring** revenues, not one-time buy

Figure 12.4. Simple perspectives to keep in mind.

At this point, each of these points should require little or no elaboration. This is the kind of thinking that makes Google, Amazon, Facebook, and similar giants seemingly unstoppable. They've designed their entire organizations around the bolded words in figure 12.4, and there's nothing to prevent you from doing the same in your industry, your value constellation, and your competitive B2B space.

You now have your roadmap toward monetizing data in hand. Time to get to work!

Conclusion

*In digital transformation, inertia is your ultimate
competitor. You need to make change happen at a
blistering pace.*

*—Jim Heppelmann,
President and CEO, PTC, LiveWorx, 2018*

IN THE INTRODUCTION AND in chapter 1, we said that the
whole premise of this book is to help companies redefine their
monetization process. What you've read so far is neither a book
on data, data transformation, and the technical side of business,
nor a book on digital transformation. Everything you've read in
this book makes up the data monetization process. Our intention
was to focus on go-to-market strategies for data-enabled offers.
We believe this is where much more attention and investments
are needed. Some of the best-in-class industrial and B2B companies that have been working in digital activities for over ten years
still struggle to move from anecdotes to data. While success in
the SaaS area is well established, go-to-market success in new

269

digital business models (e.g., IoT, IIoT, predictive maintenance) is not compelling. Recent publications and conference presentations still focus on end-use success stories without clear monetization results. These anecdotes are a blend of internal and external case studies that show the power of data-enabled applications but do not specifically address the monetization and pricing models. In fact, it's rare to find robust and generalizable digital success stories. Why is this the case? After billions in investments and a decade of hard work, why are we still stuck in anecdotes and mixed results? We posit that some of the critical barriers in digital success come from the people and cultures in these industrial organizations.

Data monetization doesn't happen without people. That makes change inevitable and far-reaching, if nothing else than because working with data is new to many B2B companies. Most are only getting started now. They have to realize that innovating in the market for data-enabled services requires people with the right skills, competencies, ambitions, opportunities, and incentives. Such people and traits are in short supply or nonexistent in most traditional (core) businesses. You have to identify and then close gaps as quickly as possible. To deploy the Data Monetization Roadmap successfully, you need multidisciplinary teams who learn and act faster than the competition in markets where technology seems to advance at the speed of light.

Adding the *people* ingredient to the data mix

The most successful digital factories and incubators—like most successful ERP deployments—are managed by businesspeople They design and lead these initiatives with the support of strong technology professionals. But putting businesspeople in charge remains a challenge. Francesco Sortino, project engineer at Ce ada, explains that one of the biggest barriers to success is that dat "is still confined in an abstract world" and that digital "is still confined to geeks." The answer, in his view, lies in "humanizing the data" by bringing in people who can turn data into commercial solutions rather than leaving the decisions up to those who collect, analyze, and interpret data.

However, the development of data-enabled services is not business as usual. The role of digital incubators and factories is to process the pipeline of data-driven ideas and to uncover the most promising opportunities. You must do the homework and apply innovative tools in the process of framing your go-to-market approach. Digital teams need to be focused on the unique opportunities that will lead to differentiated offers that customers will embrace. That potentially means that only one out of every 10 or 20 MVPs should make it out of the funnel and be commercially launched. Steve Jobs said it best: "Sometimes, when you innovate, you make mistakes. It is best to admit them quickly, and get on with improving your innovations."

Validating your hypotheses and focusing on pricing are two other important aspects of this innovation process. Most industrial natives are investing hundreds of millions in digital. Chances are that 95 to 99 percent of this money is invested in technology and operations and very little in go-to-market activities such as customer research, competitive analysis, value modeling, end-use pilots, and business planning. Is this the right approach? Or is this a case of follow-the-leader or imitation because we're all in a hurry to be in digital? The point is that making digital investments based solely on customer anecdotal evidence is no longer acceptable. As UK physician and scientist Ben Goldacre says: "The plural of *anecdote* is not *data*." You cannot base your framing work on thin air composed of customer and end-use anecdotes. Data is the new gold, but you need to validate your go-to-market hypotheses with data as well. Your go-to-market framing process needs proper financing for training, research, consulting, and other areas that build the bridges between great data-driven ideas and data-enabled solutions.

Pricing in a broad sense also needs to be part of your framing process. Yet perhaps only 15 to 20 percent of all B2B industrial companies use the value-based methodology. If you're doing cost-plus in your core business (as most do), you'll most likely do cost-plus in your digital framing as well. That must change, and the problems to address are more people-driven than data-driven:

- **Not knowing your customers.** We've preached customer intimacy throughout this book and even devoted a full chapter to it. Customer intimacy is central to the generation, testing, commercialization, and scaling of any idea. Do you have teams with the necessary skills and expertise to spend months with your customers, ask the right questions, think between the lines, and make valid and useful interpretations that lead to solutions?

- **Not knowing your competitors.** This is vitally important for so many reasons. Among them: your dollarization work is always relative, meaning that it's never sufficient to know merely how good you are. The key question is always how much *better* or *worse* you are, on a feature-by-feature as well as an aggregate basis. Also, your customers will be seeking alternatives. You need to know whom they are looking at and why. There's a reason why they call this process competitive *intelligence* and not competitive *data*.

The process needs to include value management, pricing research, price setting and price getting, and change management related to pricing. If you're not focusing on these areas, then your de facto pricing strategy is cost-plus. This is a huge mistake in th rapidly emerging world in which services dominate and hardware is no longer the priority.

This leads us to figure 13.1, which lists the red flags of data monetization.

Red flags of data monetization

The need to add the human element to the data mix leads us to the final section of our book, namely a set of red flags to watch out for during the data monetization process.

You'll notice that the bold words in figure 13.1 are all human focused rather than based on data or technology. You need people with the skills to embrace and pursue customer intimacy and to understand the nature and root causes of pains and gains. The job to be done is ultimately defined by people, not derived from data. The parallel, as we mentioned in the previous section, is competitive intelligence. You need to put your own potential solution in relative context rather than think that the entire market consists of you or "do nothing." These two aspects flow into the dollarization

---

The data monetization red flags

- Not enough customer **intimacy** and not focusing on customer jobs/pains ("techno push")
- Focused only on the "do nothing" and not knowing the next best alternatives (**NBCA**)
- Not doing any **dollarization** preparation
- Need a digital pricing **expert** for innovative pricing model design and execution
- A **culture** still deeply rooted in the hardware, "box-pushing," and cost

Figure 13.1. Five things that will make data monetization difficult to achieve.

preparation, which again requires judgment and decision making and not merely quantitative expertise.

You also need a team of pricing experts, and, once again, pricing expertise arises from a mix of qualitative skills, quantitative skills, and experience not commonly found in the same person. We strongly suggest that you seek and retain people with that mix, no matter where you find them: at consulting firms, in other industries more advanced in data monetization, or even within your own ranks.

Finally, we end with the word *culture*. The "hardware" culture carries a lot of ballast that will slow down or impede your organization. This includes everything from slow, hierarchical decision making to cost pricing to a sales culture powered by volume rather than value. You need to cut that ballast loose before it slows you down so much that your competitors sail past you and disappear over the horizon ... with your customers on board!

Authors

Stephan M. Liozu, PhD

Stephan M. Liozu is Chief Value Officer of the Thales Group (www.thalesgroup.com) and Chief Marketing Officer of Thales North America. He is also the founder of Value Innoruption Advisors, a consulting company focused on B2B value management, value-based pricing, and data monetization located in Phoenix, AZ (http://valueinnoruption.com/). He is also an adjunct professor and research fellow at Case Western Research University's Weatherhead School of Management.

Stephan holds a PhD in Management from Case Western Reserve University (2013), an MS in Innovation Management from Toulouse School of Management (2005), and an MBA in Marketing from Cleveland State University (1991). He is a Certified Pricing Professional (CPP), a Prosci® certified Change Manager, and a Strategyzer Business Model Innovation Coach.

Over the past few years, Stephan has published academic articles in the *Journal of Revenue & Pricing Management, Business Horizons, MIT Sloan Management Review,* and *Industrial Marketing Management.* He has also written several articles on strategic pricing issues for the *Journal of Professional Pricing* and is a regular presenter at Professional Pricing Society conferences in Europe and North America and at conferences of the Strategic Account Management Association. He has authored four books: *Value Mindset* (2017), *Dollarizing Differentiation Value* (2016), *The Pricing Journey* (2015), and *Pricing and Human Capital* (2015). He has also co-edited three books: *Innovation in Pricing— Contemporary Theories and Best Practices* (2012/2017), *The ROI of Pricing* (2014), and *Pricing and the Salesforce* (2015).

Wolfgang Ulaga, PhD

Wolfgang Ulaga is a marketing professor on the faculty of INSEAD, one of the world's leading and largest graduate business schools, with campuses in Europe, Asia, and the Middle East. He works with firms, executives, and students around the globe on improving their competencies and skills in marketing and sales of products, services, and customer solutions, with an emphasis on B2B markets.

His executive education and teaching activities focus on companies to (co-)create value for (and with) B2B customers, capture value through better pricing, strategically compete through service excellence, grow digital service businesses, translate data and analytics in revenues and profits, and differentiate from competition through outstanding customer experiences in professional services and industrial goods markets. For more than 20 years, he has been a frequent keynote speaker and has consulted with companies in diverse industries and designed and delivered customized executive education programs for corporations in a broad cross-section of industries and professional services markets.

Dr. Ulaga holds a PhD from the University of Paris 1 Panthéon-Sorbonne and received a Honorary Doctorate from Turku School of Economics, Finland, for his pioneering research on customer value and servitization strategies in B2B. His research investigates how firms implement value-based marketing and sales, craft service-growth strategies, develop new service business models in emerging and mature markets, design B2B service portfolios, capture more value through better service pricing, and manage the change from a product-centric to a service-savvy salesforce.

He has published numerous articles in leading academic and managerial journals, including *Harvard Business Review, Journal of Marketing, Journal of the Academy of Marketing Science,* and *Journal of Service Research,* among many others. Wolfgang has received numerous awards and recognitions, including the 2010 HEC Paris Best Teacher of the Year Award, the 2011 American Marketing Association's Winter Educators' Conference Overall Best Paper Award, the Case Centre's Annual Awards for globally best-selling case in Marketing (2015 and 2016), Top 40 Best-Selling Case Authors (2016), and the Outstanding Case Writer Award (2016).

Prior to joining INSEAD, he was on the full-time faculties at Arizona State University (Phoenix), IMD Business School (Lausanne), HEC School of Management (Paris), ESCP-EAP (Paris) and EDHEC (Lille). He also served as a Visiting Professor at the Mendoza College of Business, University of Notre Dame, Indiana.

Before beginning his career in academia, he worked in Frankfurt and Paris as a consultant for DML & Associés, an international management consulting firm.

Contributors

ConnectedValue

ConnectedValue (www.connected-value.com) is an independent professional services firm that specializes in partnering with manufacturers and industrial users of connected machines and equipment in designing, implementing, piloting, and operating equipment-as-a-service. They view the connectedness of modern machinery as an opportunity to create and price value and to share the objectives of their partners to create rapid prototypes followed by sound and scalable structures. The firm brings in

- experience in industrial solutions offerings
- solutions for administration, billing, and invoicing
- refinancing structures to realize "true sales"

Experts in Value

Experts in Value (www.expertsinvalue.com) is a consultancy that helps companies sell, market, price, and negotiate based on measurable value. They focus on strategies for sales and marketing programs, strategic account management, customer value partnership agreements, TCO procurement strategies, and a value management program called Total Profit Added™. The company is led by Todd Snelgrove, former global vice president of value at SKF and former vice president of marketing for ABB.

LeveragePoint Innovations, Inc.

LeveragePoint (https://www.leveragepoint.com/) offers a software-as-a-service solution that aligns product, pricing, marketing, sales enablement, and sales teams around creating, capturing, and communicating value. LeveragePoint allows teams to collaborate internally around building a value-based strategy and then publishing a customer-facing, dynamic, value proposition that clearly communicates the value of their offering in the first customer meeting. Global enterprises deploy LeveragePoint to make better product development and launch decisions, to implement value-based pricing, and to have better interactive customer value conversations.

Katie Richardson

Katie Richardson is a business model designer with over 20 years of experience in innovation, technology, and business model generation (Strategyzer, The Shared Clarity System™, Signals Canvas Value Canvas). She has worked for both Fortune 500 and technology startups in the areas of IIoT, Industry 4.0, and Manufacturing as a Service (MaaS). Katie focuses on business models, value propositions, and value-based pricing of technology solutions. She can be reached at https://www.linkedin.com/in/katie-richardso-890b149/.

Value Innoruption Advisors

Value Innoruption Advisors (http://valueinnoruption.com/) is a boutique consulting firm specializing in data monetization, value-based pricing, B2B pricing, and business model design. Located in Phoenix, AZ, they help industrial and B2B firms translate their marketing and digital strategies into actionable value and pricing strategies. Their methodologies include the Data Monetization framework, the Pricing Model Innovation Canvas, and the Customer Value Modeling (CVM®) certification process.

Ulaga & Associés

Ulaga & Associés is a management consulting firm in France that helps industrial and professional services companies around the globe achieve marketing and commercial excellence in B2B industries. Ulaga & Associés focuses on value-based marketing, pricing and sales—with a special emphasis on customer experience design, business model and service innovation, service-growth strategies and service portfolios development, service pricing, and product-to-service salesforce transformation. Over time, the company has served customers in a broad variety of industries, such as aerospace; agrochemicals and seeds; agricultural, construction, and forestry machinery; chemicals; construction materials; energy; food ingredients; heavy machinery; industrial gases; material handling; logistics and transportation; medical devices; mining; packaging; recycling and waste treatment; retailing; steel; and telecommunications, among others.